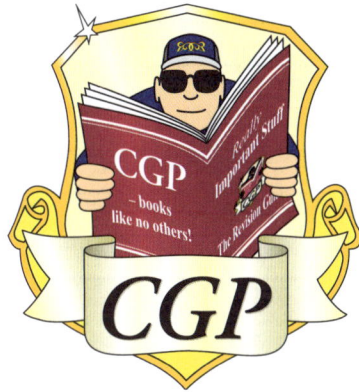

Beef up your revision muscles with CGP!

It's not easy to rack up a high score in GCSE PE — and the new Grade 9-1 course is tougher than ever. Luckily, help is at hand...

This brilliant CGP Revision Guide explains everything you need to know for the AQA exams, from dorsiflexion to data analysis! There are also plenty of exam-style questions to test you on what you've learned.

We've also included advice on how to pick up as many marks as possible, so you'll be ready to tackle your exams and finish with style.

CGP — still the best! ☺

Our sole aim here at CGP is to produce the highest quality books — carefully written, immaculately presented and dangerously close to being funny.

Then we work our socks off to get them out to you — at the cheapest possible prices.

Contents

Section Five — Sport, Society and Culture

Section Six — Health, Fitness and Well-being

Section Seven — Using Data

Published by CGP

From original material by Paddy Gannon.

Editors:
Laura Collins, Liam Dyer, William Garrison, Alison Palin and Dave Ryan.

With thanks to Chris Cope and Karen Wells for the proofreading.

With thanks to Emily Smith for the copyright research.

Definition of health on page 20 is from the preamble to the Constitution of the World Health Organization, as adopted by the International Health Conference, New York, 19 June - 22 July 1946; signed on 22 July 1946 by the representatives of 61 States (Official Records of the World Health Organization, no. 2, p.100), and entered into force on 7 April 1948.

Normative data table for grip dynamometer test on page 26 was published in 'Physical Education and the Study of Sport' 4th ed, 2002, Davis ed, p.123, 1 table ('Normative data table for grip strength test' for 16 to 19 year olds), Copyright Elsevier (2016).

Normative data for 35 m sprint test on page 26 from VCE Physical Education 2 by ARKINSTALL, M et al. (2010). Malaysia: Macmillan. p.250. Reproduced by permission of Macmillan Education Australia.

Graph of participation rates in sports on page 46 based on data from Sport England.

Source for data about shirt sponsorship in the Premier League on page 48: sportingintelligence.com.

ISBN: 978 1 78908 009 4
Printed by Elanders Ltd, Newcastle upon Tyne.
Clipart from Corel®

The Skeletal System

Welcome to the GCSE PE fun bus — first stop is the skeleton. It gives the body its shape and has loads of jobs to do. It's made up of various kinds of bones, all with their own function. Here we go...

The Skeleton has Different Functions

The skeleton does more than you might think to help your performance in sport. Its main functions are:

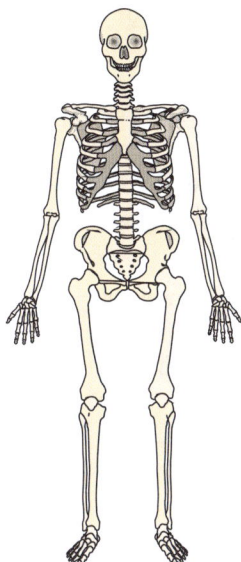

① SUPPORT/SHAPE:
1) The skeleton is a rigid bone frame for the rest of the body. Our shape is mainly due to our skeleton.
2) The skeleton supports the soft tissues like skin and muscle.
3) This helps you to have good posture, which is essential in loads of sports.
4) E.g. good posture aids performance in gymnastics.

③ MOVEMENT:
1) Muscles, attached to bones by tendons, can move bones at joints.
2) This movement is essential for good performance in sport.
3) There are different types of movement at the various joints, which are important in different sports.

② PROTECTION:
1) Bones are very tough — they protect vital organs like the brain, heart and lungs.
2) This allows you to perform well in sport without fear of serious injury.
3) E.g. the skull protects the brain, so you can head a football or take punches in a boxing match without serious injury.

④ MAKING BLOOD CELLS:
1) Some bones contain bone marrow, which makes the components of blood — red and white blood cells (see p8).
2) Red blood cells are really important during exercise — they transport the oxygen that muscles need to move.
3) Athletes with more red blood cells perform better — more oxygen can be delivered to their muscles.

⑤ MINERAL STORAGE:
1) Bones store minerals like calcium and phosphorus.
2) These help with bone strength — so you're less likely to break a bone.
3) They're also needed for muscle contraction — so the body can move.

There are Different Types of Bone in the Skeleton

There are three main types of bone in the skeleton. Each type is suited to a different purpose.

Long Bones
Long bones (e.g. the humerus in the arm) are used for larger gross movements.

Short Bones
Short bones are used for smaller fine movements — e.g. bones in the hand moving at the wrist.

Short bones are also weight-bearing — e.g. the talus in the foot supports the weight of the body. Long bones can be used as lever arms (see p17) and are strong, e.g. moving the leg at the hip.

Flat Bones
Flat bones (e.g. the ribs) protect internal organs. Their broad surface also allows muscle attachment.

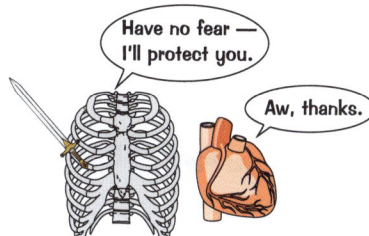

Have no fear — I'll protect you.

Aw, thanks.

I bet you found that all extremely humerus...

It's really important that you remember all the different functions of the skeleton, and how each one helps your performance in physical activity and sport. Have a go at this Exam Practice Question to test your knowledge.

Q1 Explain **one** way that the skeleton's mineral storage function aids performance in physical activity and sport.

[2 marks]

The Skeletal System

Time for some more skeleton-related fun — this page'll give you a hand at remembering the names of some important bones in the body, their types and what they do. I bet you can hardly wait...

Learn the Structure of the Skeleton

Luckily, you don't need to know all 206 bones in the human body — just some of the main ones. But you might be asked to give an example of a sporting movement that uses a particular type of bone.

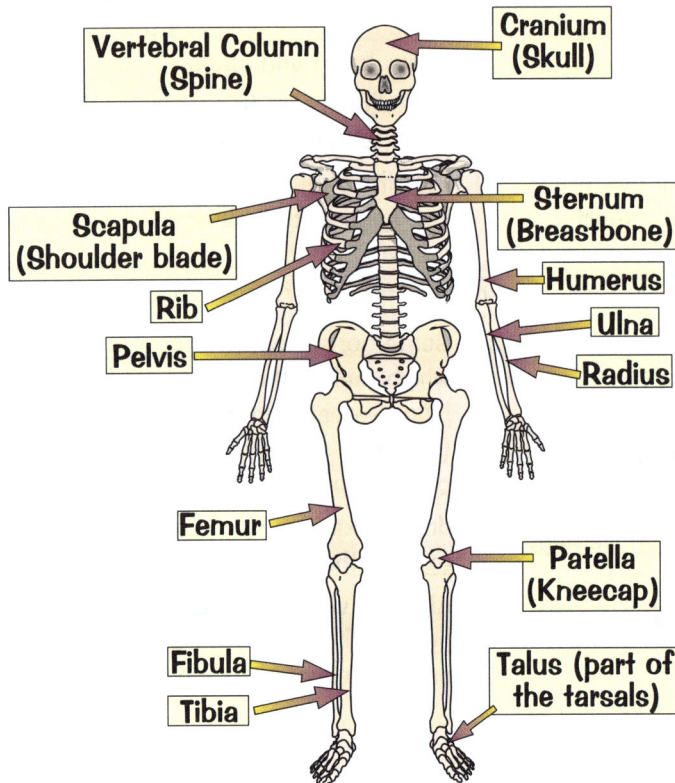

Vertebral Column (Spine) · Cranium (Skull) · Scapula (Shoulder blade) · Rib · Pelvis · Sternum (Breastbone) · Humerus · Ulna · Radius · Femur · Patella (Kneecap) · Fibula · Tibia · Talus (part of the tarsals)

Long Bones

Humerus — used by muscles to move the whole arm, e.g. swinging a badminton racket.

Ulna and radius — used by muscles to move the lower arm, e.g. bending at the elbow to throw a netball.

Femur — used by muscles to move the whole leg, e.g. when walking or running.

Fibula and tibia — used by muscles to move the lower leg, e.g. to kick a football.

Flat Bones

Cranium — protects the brain.

Sternum and ribs — protect the heart and lungs. The ribs also protect the kidneys.

Scapula — protects the shoulder joint and has many muscles attached to it, helping arm and shoulder movement.

Pelvis — protects the reproductive organs and the bladder. It also has many muscles attached to it, helping leg movement.

Short Bones

Talus — bears the body's weight when on foot, e.g. during standing and running. It is part of a group of bones called the tarsals.

Other Bones

The vertebral column (spine) is made up of irregular bones called vertebrae that protect the spinal cord.

The patella is a sesamoid bone. It protects the tendon that crosses the knee joint by stopping it rubbing against the femur.

Fluffy had a great time at the museum of natural history.

Cranium, scapulas, patellas and toes, patellas and toes...

... Not quite as catchy. Now you know all about the skeleton's structure, give these Exam Practice Questions a go.

Q1 Which **one** of these bones is found in the lower leg? **A** Femur **B** Pelvis **C** Ulna **D** Tibia [1 mark]

Q2 Which **one** of these bones is a short bone? **A** Humerus **B** Tibia **C** Talus **D** Pelvis [1 mark]

The Skeletal System

Joints are really important parts of the skeleton — you need to know what they are, how they can move and what types of joints you'll find in the body. Luckily, all that is right here on this page.

There are Different Kinds of Joint Movement

1) Joints are any points where two or more bones meet. The bones that meet at a joint are called the articulating bones of the joint.

2) Here are a few examples of some of the major joints in the body, and their articulating bones:

3) There are eight joint movements that you need to know:

Hip — pelvis and femur
Shoulder — humerus and scapula
Knee — femur and tibia
Ankle — tibia, fibula and talus
Elbow — humerus, radius and ulna

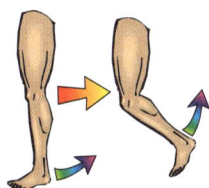

FLEXION
Closing a joint, e.g. the elbow in preparation for a basketball throw.

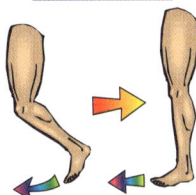

EXTENSION
Opening a joint, e.g. kicking a football.

ADDUCTION
Moving towards an imaginary centre line, e.g. swinging a golf club.

ABDUCTION
Moving away from an imaginary centre line, e.g. taking back a tennis racket before swinging it.

ROTATION
Clockwise or anticlockwise movement of a limb, e.g. the shoulder movement during a top spin forehand in tennis.

CIRCUMDUCTION
Movement of a limb, hand or foot in a circular motion, e.g. bowling a cricket ball overarm.

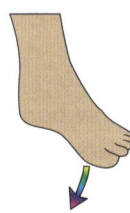

PLANTAR FLEXION
Extension at the ankle, e.g. pointing the toes during gymnastics.

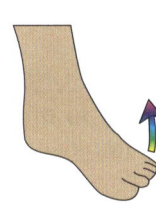

DORSIFLEXION
Flexion at the ankle, e.g. lifting the toes during gymnastics.

There are Different Joint Types in the Body

You need to know about two types of joint — ball and socket and hinge. Each type allows a certain range of movements.

type	examples	flexion and extension	adduction and abduction	rotation	circumduction
ball and socket	hip, shoulder	✓	✓	✓	✓
hinge	knee, ankle, elbow	✓	✗	✗	✗

Plantar flexion and dorsiflexion are the names for extension and flexion at the ankle.

Two bones meet at a joint — they have an excellent time together...

Make sure you learn all these joint and movement types for your exam. Now have a go at this Practice Question...

Q1 State **one** type of movement that can occur at a ball and socket joint and give an example of how it's used in a sport of your choice.

[2 marks]

The Skeletal System

Coming up on this page — a little more on joint movements, as well as what joints are made of. Spoiler alert — they're made of more than just bones. Sorry to ruin the surprise of it all...

Sports use Lots of Different Movement Types

During exercise, you'll usually use a combination of movement types, and often a combination of joints, either at the same time, or one after another. For example:

1) To do a push-up at the gym or a football throw-in, first you use flexion at the elbow to bend your arms. To straighten your arms again and complete the movements, you extend your arms at the elbow.

2) Running, kicking, basic squats and standing vertical jumps all use flexion and extension at the hip and knee. They also use plantar flexion and dorsiflexion at the ankle.

3) Bowling in cricket involves the movement of the arm in a circular motion at the shoulder. This action uses circumduction of the shoulder.

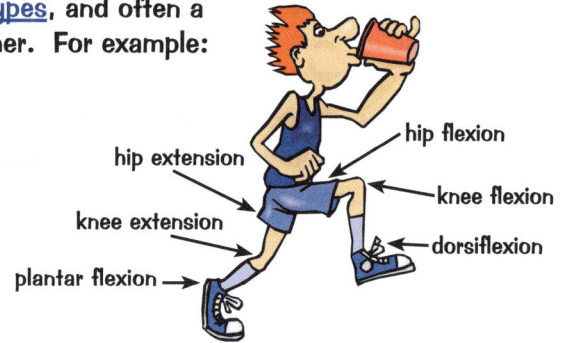

hip extension
hip flexion
knee extension
knee flexion
plantar flexion
dorsiflexion

Connective Tissues Join Muscle and Bones

There are three types of connective tissue you need to know about:

LIGAMENTS — hold bones together to restrict how much joints can move. This helps maintain the stability of the skeleton and prevents dislocation of joints. They're made of tough and fibrous tissue (like very strong string).

Ligaments also protect bones and joints by absorbing shock.

TENDONS — attach muscles to bones (or to other muscles) to allow bones to move when muscles contract.

CARTILAGE — acts as a cushion between bones to prevent damage during joint movement. It also aids the stability of a joint.

Learn the Structure of a Synovial Joint

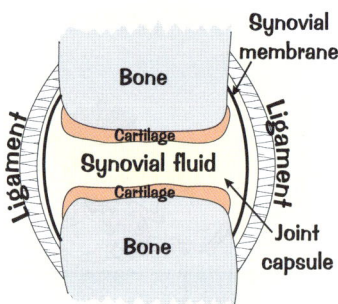

Synovial membrane
Bone
Ligament
Cartilage
Synovial fluid
Cartilage
Bone
Ligament
Joint capsule

Ball and socket and hinge joints are synovial joints. A synovial joint is a joint that allows a wide range of movement and has a joint capsule enclosing and supporting it.

1) The bones at a synovial joint are held together by ligaments.

2) The ends of the bones are covered with cartilage and are shaped so that they fit together and can move smoothly.

3) The synovial membrane releases synovial fluid into the joint capsule to lubricate (or 'oil') the joint, allowing it to move more easily.

4) Most synovial joints also have sacs of fluid called bursae (one is a 'bursa') which reduce friction between bones and tissues in and around the joint.

5) This structure helps to prevent injury to the bones that make up your joints.

All this talk about joints is making me really hungry...

Those connective tissues are really important — they all help your performance in physical activity and sport in a different way. Here are another couple of Exam Practice Questions on joints for you to have a go at.

Q1 Analyse the movement that occurs at the elbow joint during a pass in netball. [2 marks]

Q2 Explain the impact of cartilage on performance in physical activity and sport. [3 marks]

The Muscular System

The skeleton needs muscles to move the body — together these are known as the musculo-skeletal system.

Learn the Name and Function of These Muscles

BICEPS — flexion at the elbow, e.g. when curling weights.

TRICEPS — extension at the elbow, e.g. during a jump shot in basketball.

PECTORALS — adduction and flexion (horizontally) at the shoulder, e.g. during a forehand drive in tennis.

HAMSTRINGS — flexion at the knee, e.g. bringing the foot back before kicking a football.

QUADRICEPS — extension at the knee, e.g. when performing a drop kick in rugby.

GASTROCNEMIUS — plantar flexion at the ankle, e.g. standing on the toes in ballet pointe work.

Labels: pectorals, deltoids, biceps, rotator cuff, triceps, latissimus dorsi, hip flexors, abdominals, quadriceps, gluteals, hamstrings, tibialis anterior, gastrocnemius (calf)

HIP FLEXORS — flexion of the leg at the hip, e.g. lifting the knee when sprinting.

DELTOID — flexion, extension, abduction or circumduction at the shoulder. E.g. during front crawl in swimming.

TIBIALIS ANTERIOR — dorsiflexion at the ankle, e.g. during a heel side turn in snowboarding.

ABDOMINALS — flexion at the waist, e.g. during a sit-up.

GLUTEALS — extension, rotation, and abduction of the leg at the hip, e.g. pushing the body forward when running.

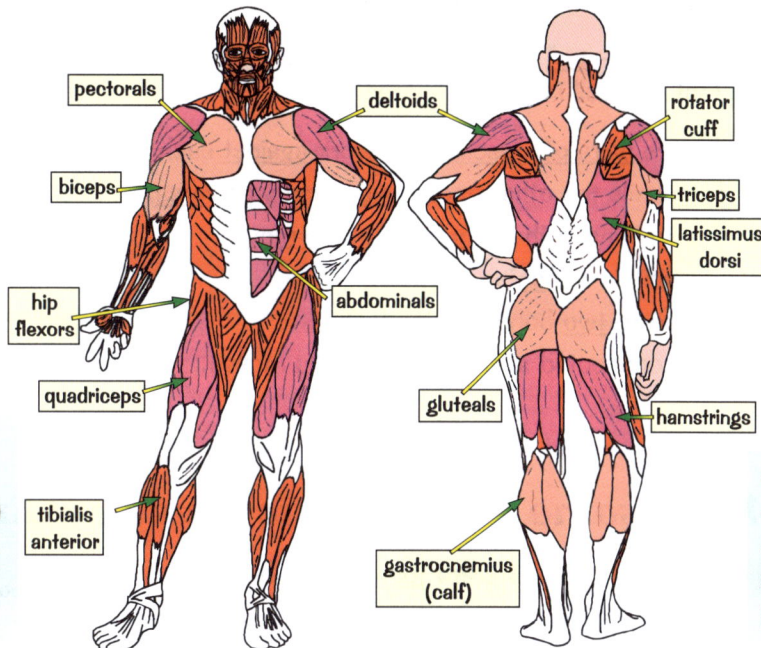

LATISSIMUS DORSI — extension, adduction or rotation at the shoulder, e.g. during butterfly stroke in swimming.

ROTATOR CUFFS — rotation and abduction at the shoulder, e.g. lifting the arms when preparing to dive. They also stabilise the shoulder joint during other movements.

There are Different Types of Muscle Contraction

When a muscle contracts, it creates tension to apply force to a bone.
Muscle contractions can be isometric or isotonic.

ISOMETRIC CONTRACTION
The muscle stays the same length, and so nothing moves.

Like if you pull on a rope attached to a wall.

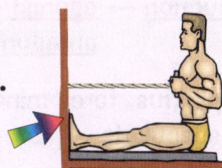

ISOTONIC CONTRACTION
The muscle changes length and so something moves.

Like if you exercise with weights that are free to move.

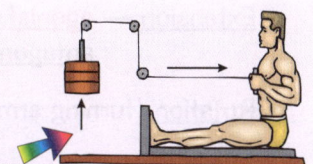

There are also two types of isotonic contraction — concentric and eccentric.

CONCENTRIC CONTRACTION
This is when a muscle contracts and shortens. This type of contraction pulls on a bone to cause a movement to happen. E.g. during the upward phase of a biceps curl, your biceps undergoes a concentric contraction to pull your forearm and lift the weight.

ECCENTRIC CONTRACTION
This is when a muscle contracts and lengthens. This helps you to control the speed of a movement. E.g. during the downward phase of a biceps curl, your biceps contracts eccentrically, creating tension so that the weight falls slowly.

Section One — Anatomy and Physiology

The Muscular System

Now on to more stuff about muscles — just what we were all hoping for. This page'll look at how muscles <u>work together</u> to produce different movement types at the <u>joints</u> in the body.

Antagonistic Muscles *Work in Pairs*

Muscles can only do one thing — <u>pull</u>. To make a joint move in two directions, you need <u>two muscles</u> that can pull in <u>opposite directions</u>.

1) <u>Antagonistic</u> muscles are <u>pairs of muscles</u> that work <u>against</u> each other.
2) One muscle <u>contracts</u> while the other one <u>relaxes</u>, and <u>vice versa</u>.
3) The muscle that's contracting is the <u>agonist</u> or <u>prime mover</u>.
4) The muscle that's relaxing is the <u>antagonist</u>.
5) Each muscle is attached to <u>two</u> bones by <u>tendons</u>.
6) Only <u>one</u> of the bones connected at the joint actually moves.

Here, 'contracts' means 'shortens', and 'relaxes' means 'lengthens'. But you might see 'contracts' used to mean 'creates tension' — which muscles do when they shorten and lengthen (see previous page).

You need to know some *Antagonistic Muscle Pairs*

There are <u>antagonistic muscle pairs</u> at different <u>joints</u> in the body:

Biceps contracts / **Triceps relaxes** / **Triceps contracts** / **Biceps relaxes**

KNEE
<u>Flexion</u> — <u>agonist</u> — hamstrings
  <u>antagonist</u> — quadriceps
<u>Extension</u> — <u>agonist</u> — quadriceps
  <u>antagonist</u> — hamstrings

ELBOW
<u>Flexion</u> — <u>agonist</u> — biceps
  <u>antagonist</u> — triceps
<u>Extension</u> — <u>agonist</u> — triceps
  <u>antagonist</u> — biceps

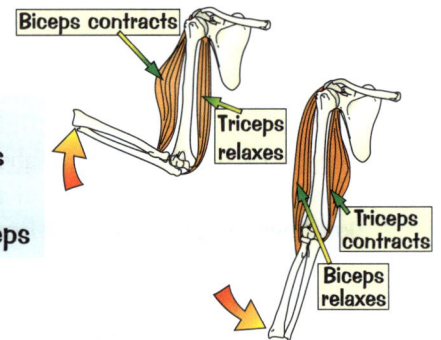

HIP
<u>Flexion</u> — <u>agonist</u> — hip flexors
  <u>antagonist</u> — gluteals
<u>Extension</u> — <u>agonist</u> — gluteals
  <u>antagonist</u> — hip flexors

ANKLE
<u>Plantar flexion</u> — <u>agonist</u> — gastrocnemius
  <u>antagonist</u> — tibialis anterior
<u>Dorsiflexion</u> — <u>agonist</u> — tibialis anterior
  <u>antagonist</u> — gastrocnemius

Other muscles are used in these shoulder movements — these are just the <u>main ones</u>.

SHOULDER
<u>Flexion</u> — <u>agonist</u> — front part of deltoid
  <u>antagonist</u> — back part of deltoid
<u>Extension</u> — <u>agonist</u> — back part of deltoid
  <u>antagonist</u> — front part of deltoid

<u>Adduction</u> — <u>agonist</u> — latissimus dorsi
  <u>antagonist</u> — middle part of deltoid
<u>Abduction</u> — <u>agonist</u> — middle part of deltoid
  <u>antagonist</u> — latissimus dorsi

<u>Rotation</u> (turning arm outwards) — <u>agonists</u> — infraspinatus, teres minor
  <u>antagonist</u> — subscapularis
<u>Rotation</u> (turning arm inwards) — <u>agonist</u> — subscapularis
  <u>antagonists</u> — infraspinatus, teres minor

The infraspinatus, teres minor and subscapularis are muscles in the <u>rotator cuffs</u> at the shoulders.

Is that a bacon rope I see? Nope, it's a hamstring...

This 'antagonistic muscle pair' stuff might seem a bit tricky, but just remember — the muscle that's the agonist in one movement will be the antagonist in the opposite movement. Here's an Exam Practice Question for you to try.

Q1 State the agonist muscle group that works to produce the hip movement when bringing the leg forward to kick a football. [1 mark]

The Cardiovascular System

Your cardiovascular system's job is to move blood around your body. As the blood travels around, it does loads of really useful stuff to help you take part in physical activity and sport. Read on to find out more...

The Cardiovascular System has Different Functions

1) The cardiovascular system helps transport things around the body in the bloodstream, like oxygen, carbon dioxide, and nutrients (e.g. glucose).

2) This gives the muscles what they need to release energy to move during exercise (and takes away any waste products).

3) When exercising, more blood is moved nearer to the skin to cool the body more quickly. This means you can exercise for a long time without overheating (see p13).

Have a look at p11 for more about how muscles use oxygen and glucose.

Learn How the Heart Pumps Blood Around the Body

1) The cardiovascular system is made up of three main parts — the heart, blood and blood vessels.

Arteries, veins and capillaries are the main types of blood vessel.

2) During any kind of physical activity, blood needs to circulate around the body to deliver oxygen and glucose to your muscles, and to take carbon dioxide away from them. This is where the heart comes in.

RIGHT SIDE

- Deoxygenated blood enters the right atrium from the vena cava (a vein) as the heart relaxes.
- The right atrium contracts, pushing the blood through a valve into the right ventricle.
- The right ventricle contracts, pushing the blood through another valve into the pulmonary artery, which carries the blood to the lungs.
- Gases are exchanged in the lungs and the blood is oxygenated (see p9 for more information).

LEFT SIDE

- Oxygenated blood enters the left atrium from the pulmonary vein as the heart relaxes.
- The left atrium contracts, pushing the blood through a valve into the left ventricle.
- The left ventricle contracts, pushing the blood through another valve into the aorta (an artery). This transports the oxygenated blood to the rest of the body — including the muscles.
- When the muscles have used the oxygen in the blood, it becomes deoxygenated again.

Each valve has a name, but you don't need to know them for the exam.

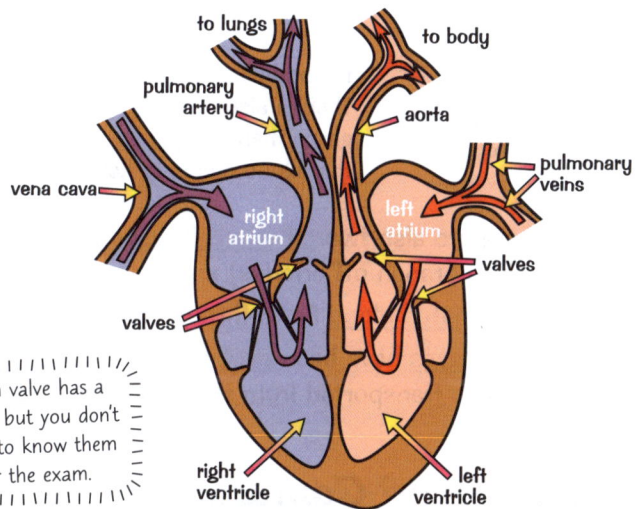

The atria (plural of atrium) and ventricles are called chambers. The heart has 4 chambers — an atrium and ventricle on each side.

3) Diastole is when the heart relaxes and fills with blood and systole is when it contracts and pumps the blood out. Both sides of the heart relax at the same time and then contract at the same time. One cardiac cycle is a phase of diastole and systole — it might help to think of this as one 'heartbeat'.

4) Blood flows because of differences in pressure caused by the cardiac cycle. Valves open to let blood fill the heart chambers, and close to prevent backflow — this is when blood flows the wrong way.

The heart — it's all just pump and circumstance...

To understand the left's and right's on the diagram, just imagine you are viewing the heart from behind. Now, get learning what all the bits of the cardiovascular system do, and try this Practice Question.

Q1 Analyse the role of the pulmonary artery in physical activity and sport. [4 marks]

8

The Cardiovascular System

Your cardiovascular system has different types of blood vessels that carry blood around your body. This page'll tell you all about them, as well as some of the wonderful stuff your blood is made of.

Arteries, Veins and Capillaries Carry Blood

1) Blood vessels transport blood — they have a hollow centre called the lumen so blood can flow through. The diameter of the lumen varies for the different types of blood vessel.

2) Blood pressure measures how strongly the blood presses against the walls of blood vessels. Blood vessels with thicker walls can carry blood at higher pressure.

3) Different types of blood vessel are suited to different roles:

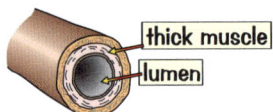

thick muscle
lumen

ARTERIES — carry blood away from the heart. All arteries carry oxygenated blood except for the pulmonary arteries. Their thick, muscular walls allow them to carry blood flowing at high pressure.

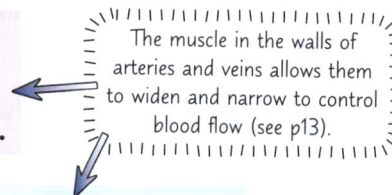

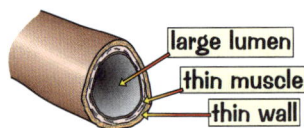

The muscle in the walls of arteries and veins allows them to widen and narrow to control blood flow (see p13).

large lumen
thin muscle
thin wall

VEINS — carry blood towards the heart. They have valves to stop blood flowing the wrong way. All veins carry deoxygenated blood, except for the pulmonary veins. They carry blood at low pressure, so they have thinner walls and less muscle than arteries.

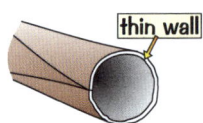

thin wall

CAPILLARIES — carry blood through the body to exchange gases and nutrients with the body's tissues. They have very thin walls so substances can easily pass through. They're also very narrow, which means lots of them can fit into the body's tissues — giving them a large surface area to let gas exchange happen more easily. It also means that blood can only flow through them slowly — giving more time for gas exchange.

4) There are also two other small types of blood vessel — arterioles (which branch off arteries) and venules (which meet to form veins).

5) Oxygenated blood flows through arteries into arterioles, then into capillaries.

6) After gases have been exchanged between the capillaries and the body tissues, blood is transported from the capillaries into venules, where it flows back into the veins.

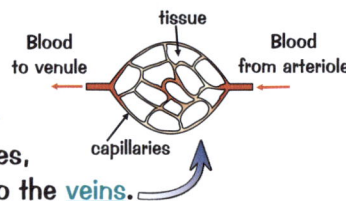

tissue
Blood to venule
Blood from arteriole
capillaries

Your Blood Contains Red and White Blood Cells

You need to know about two types of cells that make up the blood in your body. They have different jobs, which are important in helping your body to take part in physical activity.

RED BLOOD CELLS — Carry oxygen and transport it around the body to be used to release energy needed by muscles during physical activity. They also carry carbon dioxide to the lungs. Haemoglobin (a protein in red blood cells) stores the oxygen and carbon dioxide. Oxyhaemoglobin is formed by oxygen and haemoglobin combining.

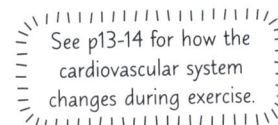

See p13-14 for how the cardiovascular system changes during exercise.

WHITE BLOOD CELLS — Fight against disease so you stay healthy and perform well.

What do vampires cross the sea in? Blood vessels...

If you're struggling to remember whether veins and arteries carry blood to or from the heart, just remember — arteries carry blood away from the heart. Here's a Practice Question for you to have a go at.

Q1 State **one** characteristic of capillaries and explain how it aids performance in physical activity and sport.　　　　　　　　　[3 marks]

Section One — Anatomy and Physiology

The Respiratory System

You'll probably recognise most of this stuff from biology — but there's no harm in a quick recap.

Learn the *Structure* of the *Respiratory System*

The respiratory system is everything you use to breathe.
It's found in the chest cavity — the area inside the chest.

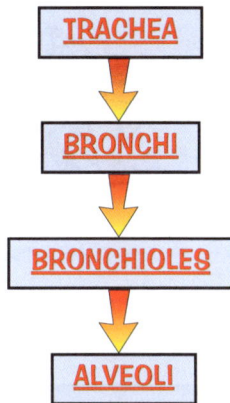

TRACHEA
⬇
BRONCHI
⬇
BRONCHIOLES
⬇
ALVEOLI

1) Air passes through the nose or mouth and then on to the trachea.

2) The trachea splits into two tubes called bronchi (each one is a 'bronchus') — one going to each lung.

3) The bronchi split into progressively smaller tubes called bronchioles.

4) The bronchioles finally end at small bags called alveoli (each one is an 'alveolus') where gases are exchanged (see below).

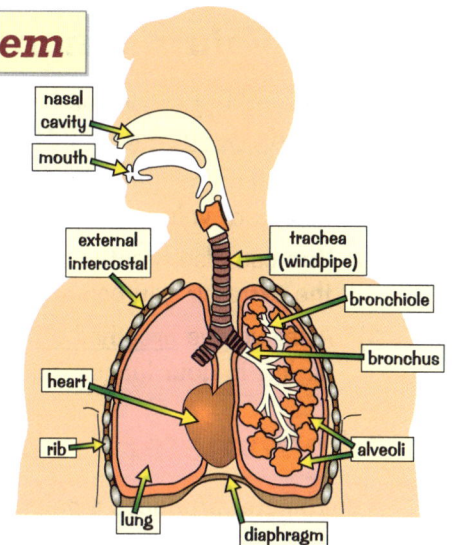

See p12 for how the respiratory system responds to exercise.

The diaphragm and external intercostal muscles help the air to move:

- When you breathe in, the diaphragm and external intercostals contract to move the ribcage upwards and expand the chest cavity. This decreases the air pressure in the lungs, drawing air in.
- When you breathe out, the diaphragm and the external intercostals relax, moving the ribcage down and shrinking the chest cavity. Air pressure in the lungs increases, forcing air out of the lungs the same way it came in.

Oxygen *and* Carbon Dioxide *are* Exchanged *in the* Alveoli

1) The cardiovascular and respiratory systems have to work together to get oxygen to the muscles, and carbon dioxide away from them. They do this by exchanging gases between the alveoli and capillaries surrounding them.

The cardiovascular and respiratory systems together make up the cardio-respiratory system.

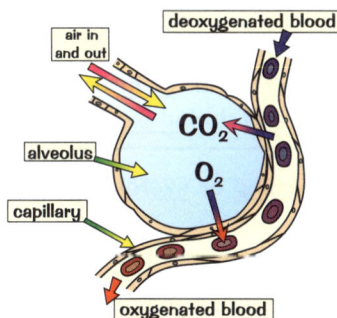

1) Oxygenated blood delivers oxygen and collects carbon dioxide as it circulates around the body. Deoxygenated blood returns to the heart and is then pumped to the lungs.

2) In the lungs, carbon dioxide moves from the blood in the capillaries into the alveoli so it can be breathed out.

3) Oxygen from the air you breathe into the lungs moves across from the alveoli to the red blood cells in the capillaries.

4) The oxygenated blood returns to the heart and is pumped to the rest of the body. The red blood cells carry the oxygen around the body and deliver it where it's needed, e.g. the muscles.

2) Alveoli are surrounded by lots of capillaries, giving them a large blood supply to exchange gases with.

3) They also have a large surface area and moist, thin walls — so gases only have a short distance to move.

4) This exchange of gases happens through a process called diffusion. This means the gases move down a concentration gradient — from a place of higher concentration to a place of lower concentration:

IN ALVEOLUS	IN CAPILLARY
High concentration of O_2	Low concentration of O_2
Low concentration of CO_2	High concentration of CO_2

DIFFUSION OF O_2 →
← DIFFUSION OF CO_2

O_2 = oxygen
CO_2 = carbon dioxide

Air we go — keeping trachea respiratory system...

So, diffusion is pretty impressive, eh? I bet you'll be impressed with this Exam Practice Question, too.

Q1 Describe how deoxygenated blood becomes oxygenated. [3 marks]

The Respiratory System

The amount of air in your <u>lungs</u> can be measured by a snazzy machine called a <u>spirometer</u>.

Tidal Volume Increases during Exercise

1) The <u>amount of air</u> you breathe in or out during <u>one breath</u> is known as your <u>tidal volume</u>. During <u>exercise</u> your tidal volume <u>increases</u> as you take <u>deeper breaths</u> (see p12).

2) After a <u>normal breath in</u>, you can still breathe in <u>more air</u> — this extra volume of air is your <u>inspiratory reserve volume</u> (IRV).

3) You can also breathe out <u>more air</u> after a <u>normal breath out</u> — the extra air you can breathe out is your <u>expiratory reserve volume</u> (ERV).

4) After you've <u>breathed out</u> as much air as you can, there's still some air <u>left</u> in your lungs. This is called the <u>residual volume</u>.

A Spirometer Trace shows Lung Air Volumes

A <u>spirometer</u> produces a graph called a <u>spirometer trace</u>, which shows the <u>volume of air</u> in your lungs.

This shows one <u>whole breath</u> in and out. The parts of the trace that go <u>up</u> are during <u>inhalation</u>. The parts that go <u>down</u> are during <u>exhalation</u>.

The <u>small changes</u> in volume show <u>normal breaths</u> in and out.

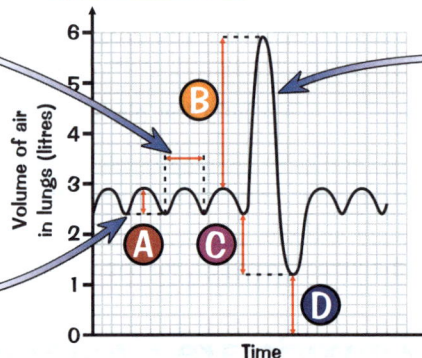

These <u>big changes</u> in volume show a <u>maximum inspiration</u> and <u>maximum expiration</u> — breathing in and out <u>as much as possible</u>.

Your IRV and ERV decrease during exercise — you're breathing in and out more air than normal, so you can't breathe in or out as much extra air.

You need to be able to read some <u>lung volumes</u> from a spirometer trace:

A The difference in volume between a 'peak' and a 'dip' shows the <u>tidal volume</u>. When you're not exercising, an <u>average</u> tidal volume is about <u>500 ml</u>.

B The difference in volume here is the <u>inspiratory reserve volume</u>. It's usually about <u>3 litres</u> when you're not exercising.

C This difference in volume gives the <u>expiratory reserve volume</u>. This is usually about <u>1.2 litres</u> when you're at rest.

D This shows the <u>residual volume</u>. It's normally around <u>1.2 litres</u> — both <u>at rest</u> and <u>during exercise</u>.

A spirometer trace can show you whether the person breathing into it was <u>resting</u> or <u>exercising</u>.

1) When you exercise, your <u>tidal volume increases</u> — you take deeper breaths in and out. So during the '<u>exercise</u>' part of the spirometer trace, the 'peaks' are <u>higher</u> and the 'dips' are <u>lower</u> than during the '<u>rest</u>' part.

2) Your <u>breathing rate</u> also increases when you exercise — you take <u>more breaths</u> per minute than when you're resting. This is shown on the spirometer trace by the 'peaks' being <u>closer together</u> during exercise.

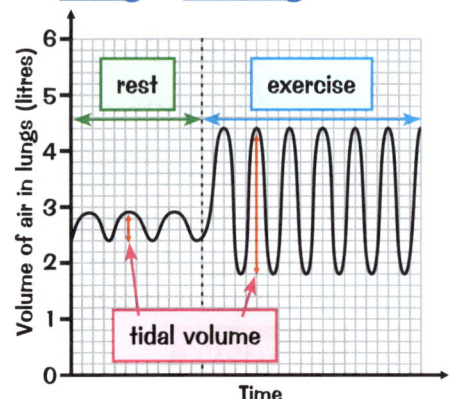

I measured my lung volumes — they sounded pretty quiet to me...

You might need to draw a spirometer trace on a set of axes in your exam. But don't panic — just remember that the 'peaks' of the trace get taller and closer together during exercise, and you'll be fine. Try this Practice Question.

Q1 Look at the lung volume 'A' on the first spirometer trace on this page. Describe any changes to this volume during exercise and how they would appear on a spirometer trace.   [2 marks]

Aerobic and Anaerobic Exercise

Your body can release energy in different ways — it all depends on how hard and how long you're exercising. And different sources of fuel can be used to release energy in the muscles. Fantastic stuff.

Aerobic Exercise — With Oxygen

1) All the living cells in your body need energy. Normally the body uses oxygen to release energy from glucose (a sugar found in food). This is called aerobic respiration.

Glucose + Oxygen ➡ Carbon dioxide + Water + Energy

Carbon dioxide and water are by-products of aerobic respiration.

2) If your body's keeping up with the oxygen demand of its cells, it means there's enough oxygen available for aerobic respiration.

3) Exercise where your body can keep up with oxygen demand is called aerobic.

> AEROBIC EXERCISE: 'with oxygen'. When exercise is not too fast and is steady, the heart can supply all the oxygen that the working muscles need.

4) You breathe out the carbon dioxide through your lungs, while the water is lost as sweat, urine, or in the air you breathe out.

5) As long as your muscles are supplied with enough oxygen, you can do aerobic exercise — so if you're exercising for long periods, you'll be producing your energy aerobically.

6) Aerobic respiration is how marathon runners get their energy — it's the most efficient way to get it.

Anaerobic Exercise — Without Oxygen

1) During vigorous exercise, your body can't supply all the oxygen needed. When this happens, your muscles release energy without using oxygen in a different process called anaerobic respiration.

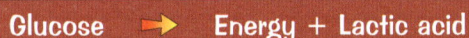

Glucose ➡ Energy + Lactic acid

Lactic acid is a by-product of anaerobic respiration — you need oxygen to remove it (see next page).

2) Exercise where your body has to do this is called anaerobic.

> ANAEROBIC EXERCISE: 'without oxygen'. When exercise duration is short and at high intensity, the heart and lungs can't supply blood and oxygen to muscles as fast as the cells need them.

3) The lack of oxygen during anaerobic respiration means it can only provide energy for short periods of time — so you can't exercise at high intensity for very long.

4) Sprinters get their energy anaerobically — they have to run quickly for short durations.

Carbohydrates and Fats are used as Fuel

1) Your body needs a source of fuel so that respiration can provide energy.

2) Carbohydrates (from foods such as pasta) and fats stored in the body can both be used as fuel.

> CARBOHYDRATES — the body's main source of fuel. They're used during aerobic exercise at moderate intensity and for high intensity anaerobic exercise.

> FATS — used as fuel for aerobic exercise at low intensity. Fats provide more energy than carbohydrates, but they can't be used as fuel for higher intensity exercise.

Have you met Anna Robic? She's an excellent sprinter...

You can adapt your training intensity based on whether you want to make your body better at exercising aerobically or anaerobically — have a look at page 29 to see how. Have a go at this Practice Question, too.

Q1 Justify why a 100 metre sprint would be an anaerobic exercise.   [3 marks]

Short-Term Effects of Exercise

Exercise has loads of different short-term effects on the body — some that help you to exercise, and others that are just a bit nasty. This page'll look at the effects on your muscles and your breathing.

There are Short-Term Effects on the Muscular System

There are loads of different effects on your muscles during exercise, and straight after it.

1) When you exercise, your muscles release extra energy for movement. Producing this energy also generates heat, which can make you feel hot and sweaty.

2) Also, during anaerobic exercise, your muscles produce lactic acid. If you use your muscles anaerobically for too long, the lactic acid starts to build up. This leads to a rise in the lactate levels in the body — lactate accumulation.

3) Lactic acid build-up makes your muscles painful and causes muscle fatigue (tiredness).

4) If your muscles are fatigued, they need oxygen to remove the lactic acid and recover. The amount of oxygen you need is the oxygen debt, or 'EPOC' — excess post-exercise oxygen consumption.

5) To repay oxygen debt, you'll need to slow down or stop the exercise you're doing for a while, which can have a negative impact on your performance.

6) During a training session where you do anaerobic exercise, you'll need to have periods of rest or low intensity exercise before you can work anaerobically again.

Working your muscles really hard during a workout can also affect your body a day or two after exercise.

1) You might feel tired because your muscles used up lots of energy during your workout.

2) You could also feel sick and light-headed.

3) Some people also get 'delayed onset of muscle soreness' (DOMS), or muscle cramp.

A cool-down (see p35) can help prevent these effects.

There are Short-Term Effects on the Respiratory System

1) During exercise, muscles such as the pectorals and the sternocleidomastoid (in the neck) expand your lungs more to let in extra air. Muscles in your abdomen also work to pull your ribcage down and shrink the chest cavity quicker, so you breathe out faster.

2) These changes help to increase your depth of breathing (which leads to an increase in your tidal volume — see p10) and rate of breathing (the number of breaths per minute).

3) This means more oxygen is taken in and transferred to the blood, which helps to meet the increased demand for oxygen in the muscles during physical activity.

4) It also helps you to breathe out the extra carbon dioxide produced during aerobic respiration.

5) These changes allow you to do aerobic exercise for long periods of time.

6) If you've been doing anaerobic exercise, your breathing rate and depth will remain higher than normal until you've taken in enough oxygen to 'pay off' your oxygen debt.

These changes to your respiratory system will all be more extreme if you exercise really intensely. So you'll breathe deeper and quicker when you're exercising hard than when you're doing light exercise.

My brainular system feels fatigued...

It's not enough just knowing that you breathe faster and deeper during exercise — you need to know why, too. So remember, you need to get extra oxygen in, and extra carbon dioxide out. Now try an Exam Practice Question.

Q1   Outline how muscle fatigue may affect a player participating in a game of football.   [1 mark]

Short-Term Effects of Exercise

Your cardiovascular system works extra hard during exercise to make sure your muscles get what they need to work properly. This includes using your blood vessels to send your blood where it's needed the most.

There are Short-Term Effects on the Cardiovascular System

1) Your heart rate is the number of times your heart beats per minute. An adult's resting heart rate (their heart rate when they aren't exercising) is usually about 60-80 bpm (beats per minute).

2) Your stroke volume is the amount of blood each ventricle pumps with each contraction (or heartbeat).

3) During exercise, your heart rate and stroke volume both increase.

4) This leads to an increase in your cardiac output — the volume of blood pumped by a ventricle per minute.

> cardiac output (Q) = heart rate × stroke volume

5) It also increases the pressure of your blood as your heart beats — your systolic blood pressure.

> Diastolic blood pressure is your blood's pressure when your heart is relaxed. It doesn't change much during exercise.

6) An increase in cardiac output increases the blood and oxygen supply to your muscles — so they can release the energy they need for physical activity. It also removes more carbon dioxide from the muscles and takes it to the lungs to be breathed out.

7) Your heart rate, stroke volume and cardiac output will remain higher than normal after exercise until any oxygen debt is paid off.

> The harder you're exercising, the higher your heart rate, stroke volume and cardiac output will be. So if you're only doing very light exercise, they'll be lower than if you were doing really strenuous exercise.

Your Blood Vessels Change when you Exercise

When you exercise, blood is redistributed around the body to increase the supply of oxygen to your muscles.

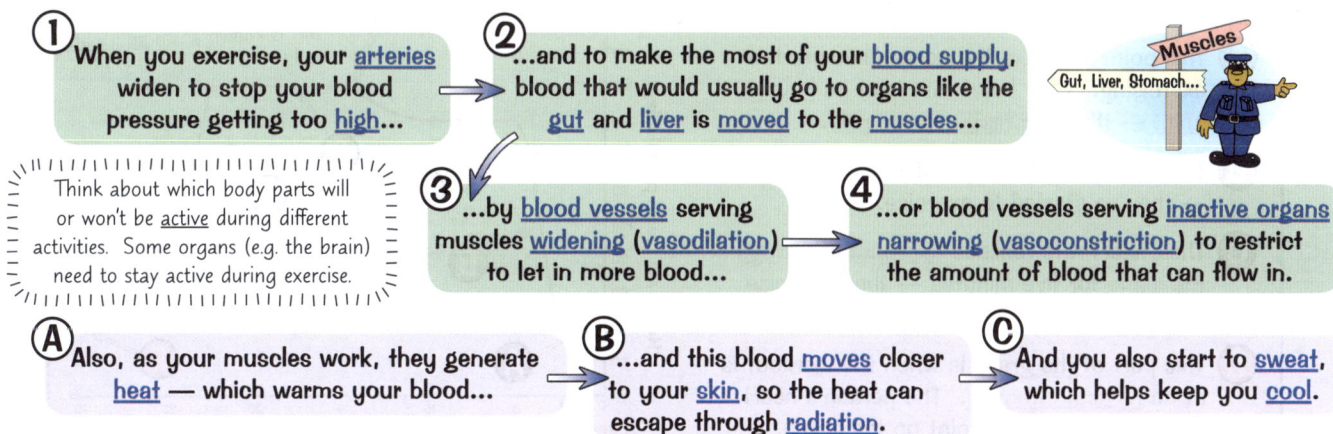

① When you exercise, your arteries widen to stop your blood pressure getting too high...

② ...and to make the most of your blood supply, blood that would usually go to organs like the gut and liver is moved to the muscles...

> Think about which body parts will or won't be active during different activities. Some organs (e.g. the brain) need to stay active during exercise.

③ ...by blood vessels serving muscles widening (vasodilation) to let in more blood...

④ ...or blood vessels serving inactive organs narrowing (vasoconstriction) to restrict the amount of blood that can flow in.

Ⓐ Also, as your muscles work, they generate heat — which warms your blood...

Ⓑ ...and this blood moves closer to your skin, so the heat can escape through radiation.

Ⓒ And you also start to sweat, which helps keep you cool.

The amount of blood that's redistributed depends on how intensely you're exercising. So during light exercise, only a small amount of blood is moved towards your working muscles. But if you're exercising really hard, a lot more blood is moved.

Romantic comedies — exercise for your heart...

Remember, blood is redistributed around the body during exercise, because your muscles need more than some of your organs. And this couldn't happen without vasodilation and vasoconstriction. Now, some Practice Questions...

Q1 State **two** short-term effects that exercise has on the cardiovascular system. [2 marks]

Q2 Katie swims continuously for 30 minutes in a swimming pool.
Explain how vasodilation helps her exercise aerobically. [3 marks]

Short-Term Effects of Exercise

This page'll show you how the cardiovascular and respiratory systems team up to help you exercise. It'll also give you some handy tips on how to interpret heart rate data that you might see in the exam.

The Cardiovascular and Respiratory Systems Work Together

1) During exercise (and immediately after), more oxygen is delivered to the muscles than normal. Extra carbon dioxide is also taken away from them and breathed out.

2) The cardiovascular and respiratory systems work together to make this happen. When you exercise:

MORE O_2 DELIVERED

1) Breathing rate and depth increase, so more oxygen is delivered to the alveoli in the lungs.

2) Cardiac output also increases — so blood passes through the lungs at a faster rate, and picks up the extra oxygen from the alveoli. It's then delivered to the muscles.

MORE CO_2 REMOVED

1) Increased cardiac output means that the blood can transport carbon dioxide from the muscles to the lungs more quickly.

2) Here it moves back into the alveoli, and the higher breathing rate and depth allow it to be quickly breathed out.

3) These changes maintain a high concentration gradient. After you breathe in, there's a lot more oxygen in the alveoli than the capillaries, and a lot more carbon dioxide in the capillaries than the alveoli.

4) This allows diffusion of the gases to happen much quicker during exercise.

5) These processes help you to release enough energy to exercise aerobically and to recover from oxygen debt after anaerobic exercise (see p12).

For more on diffusion, have a look at page 9.

Heart Rate can be shown Graphically

1) In your exam, you might get a graph or table showing a person's heart rate during a workout.

2) This increases during exercise, and gradually goes back to normal once they stop exercising.

3) You can use this fact to interpret data and work out whether the person was resting, exercising or recovering at a specific time.

Your heart rate might go up slightly just before you start exercising — this is known as an anticipatory rise.

(A) This point is before the person has started exercising. Their heart rate is at its lowest point — it's their resting heart rate.

(B) Their heart rate has started to increase — they've started to exercise.

(C) Their heart rate reaches 130 bpm and stays the same for five minutes — they exercise at the same intensity for that time.

(D) This part of the graph is when the workout is at its highest intensity. The person's heart rate is at its highest point on the graph.

(E) Their heart rate is decreasing — exercise has stopped, or they're completing a cool down. Their heart rate stays fairly high for a while to help with recovery.

(F) They've returned to their resting heart rate of 70 beats per minute.

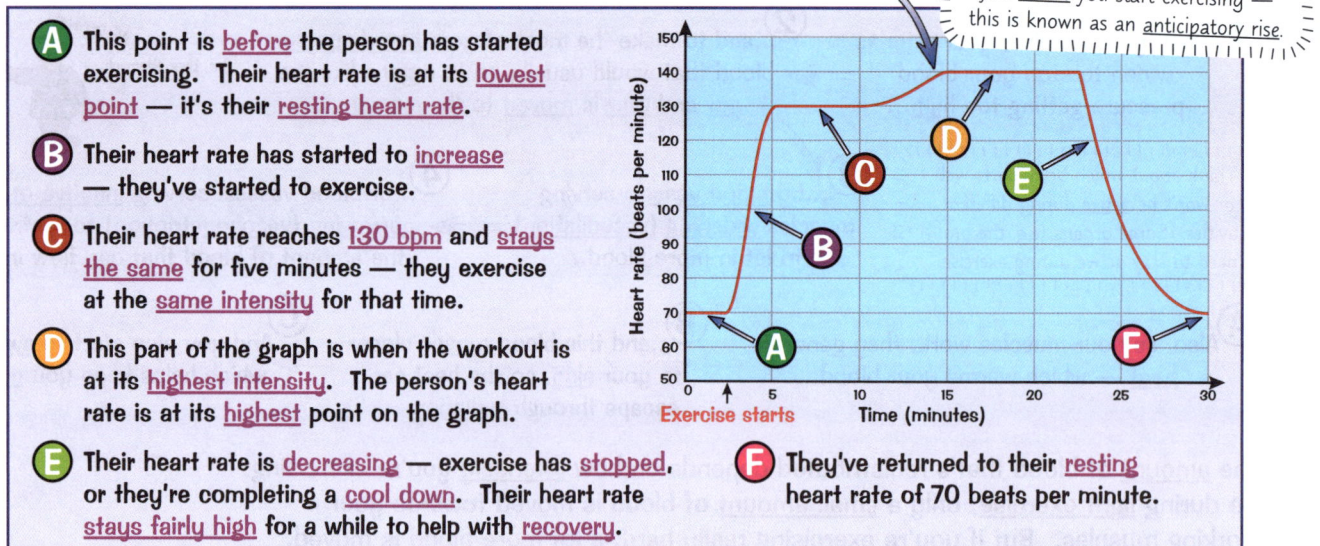

Interpreting graphs? I didn't sign up for extra maths lessons...

I bet you weren't pleased to see a graph on this page, but it's not too bad. If you get given any heart rate data in your exam, remember that it goes up during exercise and back down afterwards. Then you can work out what was going on when the values were recorded. Try this Exam Practice Question.

Q1 The table on the right shows an athlete's heart rate recorded three times during a training session. Identify which value was recorded:

| 114 bpm | 167 bpm | 53 bpm |

a) before exercise started [1 mark]   b) during high-intensity exercise [1 mark]

Long-Term Effects of Exercise

Exercising regularly eventually leads to loads of adaptations in the body's systems.
These benefit your health and different components of fitness, which will help improve your performance.

Exercise Improves the Musculo-Skeletal System

Long-term effects of exercise can take months or years to become noticeable.
There are lots of ways that regular exercise can benefit your musculo-skeletal system:

MUSCLE HYPERTROPHY

1) Doing regular exercise will make your muscles thicker and reduce the weight of your body (by using fat to supply glucose). This can change your body shape.

2) This thickening of muscles is called hypertrophy. It happens to all muscles when they're exercised, including your heart.

3) The thicker a muscle is, the more strongly it can contract — so this increases your strength.

4) Hypertrophy also improves your muscular endurance — so you can use your muscles for longer.

Boring trophy   Hypertrophy

Weight training (see p31) is a good way to make your muscles thicker.

See p54-55 for more about the long-term benefits of exercise.

STRONGER LIGAMENTS & TENDONS Having stronger ligaments and tendons means you're less likely to injure yourself, e.g. dislocation. Repeated use of muscles and joints can increase suppleness.

INCREASED SPEED Over long periods of time, intense anaerobic exercises, such as sprinting, can improve your speed, as well as help you recover more quickly after exercise.

Exercise Improves the Cardio-Respiratory System

BIGGER/STRONGER HEART

1) Your heart is just a muscle — when you exercise, it adapts and gets bigger and stronger. This is called cardiac hypertrophy.

2) A bigger, stronger heart will contract more strongly and pump more blood with each beat — so your resting stroke volume and maximum cardiac output will increase.

3) A larger stroke volume means your heart has to beat less often to pump the same amount of blood around your body. This means your resting heart rate decreases — which is called bradycardia.

Training that involves aerobic exercise works best to improve the cardio-respiratory system.

INCREASED CARDIOVASCULAR ENDURANCE / STAMINA

1) The ability to supply blood and oxygen to your muscles is known as cardiovascular endurance.

2) Aerobic exercises, such as swimming, increase your cardiovascular endurance and stamina — so you can exercise for longer.

There's more about cardiovascular endurance on p20.

Exercise can Improve Components of Fitness

You can target specific areas of fitness (see pages 20-23) to improve, for example:

- A gymnast might want to increase their suppleness, so they can perform more difficult skills (e.g. a split jump).
- A cyclist might want to increase their cardiovascular endurance, so they have the stamina to cycle long distances.

Breaking news — exercise is good for you...

To get all these lovely long-term effects, you'll need to rest after exercise so that you can recover and let your body adapt to any changes. Here's the last Exam Practice Question in this section for you to try. Have fun...

Q1   Justify why muscle hypertrophy would benefit a performer participating in weightlifting.   [3 marks]

Revision Questions For Section One

Well, that's Anatomy and Physiology all wrapped up — time to see how much you know about the body.

- Try these questions and tick off each one when you get it right.
- When you've done all the questions for a topic and are completely happy with it, tick off the topic.
- The answers can all be found by looking back over pages 1 to 15.

The Musculo-Skeletal System (p1-6) ☑

1) Name the five main functions of the skeleton. ☑
2) State the three main types of bone in the body. ☑
3) Which bones protect the heart and lungs? ☑
4) Which two bones meet to make the hip joint? ☑
5) Which joint movement involves pointing the toes upwards? ☑
6) Give an example of a hinge joint. ☑
7) What is the function of:
   a) Cartilage?
   b) Ligaments?
   c) Tendons? ☑
8) What is the function of the synovial membrane within a joint? ☑
9) Name three muscles that are found in the leg. ☑
10) What is the difference between an isometric and an isotonic muscle contraction? ☑
11) Which two muscles make up the antagonistic muscle pair operating at the elbow joint? ☑

The Cardio-Respiratory System (p7-10) ☐

12) Give two functions of the cardiovascular system. ☐
13) Which vein does deoxygenated blood pass through to enter the heart? ☐
14) The pulmonary artery carries oxygenated blood to the rest of the body. TRUE or FALSE? ☐
15) Name the three types of blood vessel found in the body. ☐
16) What is the function of red blood cells? ☐
17) Explain how gases are exchanged between the alveoli and capillaries. ☐
18) Describe what is meant by tidal volume. ☐
19) What does a spirometer measure? ☐

Aerobic and Anaerobic Exercise (p11) ☐

20) Describe aerobic and anaerobic respiration. ☐
21) Would a triathlete use aerobic respiration, anaerobic respiration, or both? ☐

The Short-Term and Long-Term Effects of Exercise (p12-15) ☐

22) Explain what EPOC is and how you can recover from it. ☐
23) Explain why your depth and rate of breathing increase during exercise. ☐
24) Why do heart rate, stroke volume and cardiac output remain higher after exercise? ☐
25) Explain what vasodilation and vasoconstriction are and why they happen. ☐
26) What is muscle hypertrophy and why does it happen? ☐
27) How does regular exercise benefit the ligaments and tendons? ☐
28) Give two long-term effects of exercise on the cardiovascular system. ☐

Lever Systems

When the muscular and skeletal systems work together, they create lever systems that help us to move.

Lever Systems Help the Body to Move

A lever is a rigid bar that moves about a fixed point when force is applied to it.
When a muscle pulls on a bone to move a body part about a joint, it uses the body part as a lever.
This lever makes up part of a lever system that has four different components:

1) The lever arm — the bone or body part being moved about a point.
   On a diagram of a lever system, it's shown as a straight line.

2) The fulcrum — the joint where the lever arm pivots. It's shown as a triangle.

3) The effort — the force applied by the muscles to the lever arm.
   It's shown by an arrow pointing in the direction of the force.

4) The load or resistance against the pull of the muscles on the lever arm. E.g. the weight of the body,
   or body part, or something being lifted. A square or an arrow is used to represent the load.

You might be asked to draw a diagram of a lever system used in a sporting movement — make sure you label the fulcrum, effort and load (see below).

There are three types of lever system:

FIRST CLASS — The load and effort are at opposite ends of the lever. The fulcrum is in the middle.	SECOND CLASS — The fulcrum and effort are at opposite ends of the lever. The load is in the middle.	THIRD CLASS — The fulcrum and load are at opposite ends of the lever. The effort is in the middle.

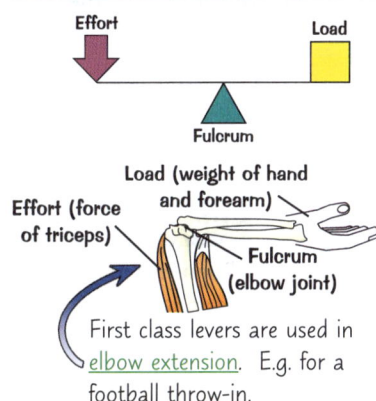

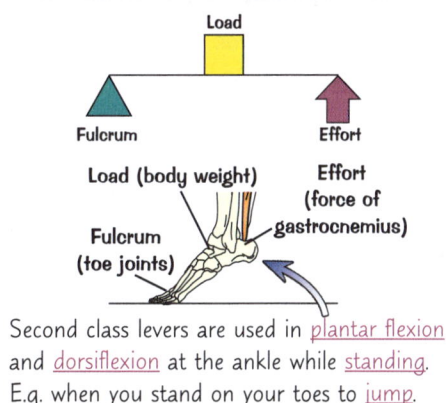

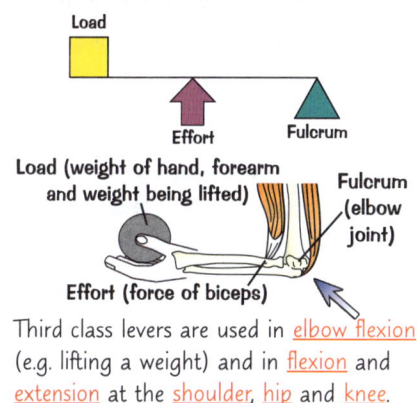

First class levers are used in elbow extension. E.g. for a football throw-in.

Second class levers are used in plantar flexion and dorsiflexion at the ankle while standing. E.g. when you stand on your toes to jump.

Third class levers are used in elbow flexion (e.g. lifting a weight) and in flexion and extension at the shoulder, hip and knee.

Levers have a Mechanical Advantage

Different levers have different benefits. The mechanical advantage of a lever measures how efficient it is at moving heavy loads. It depends on the effort arm (the distance between the fulcrum and the effort) and the weight (resistance) arm (the distance between the fulcrum and the load):

> Mechanical advantage = effort arm ÷ weight (resistance) arm

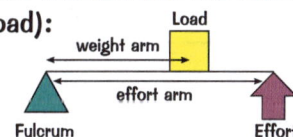

1) A lever in the body with a high mechanical advantage (a value bigger than 1) can move a large load with a small effort from the muscles. However, it can only move the load short distances at low speeds.

2) Second class levers have a high mechanical advantage — the effort arm is longer than the weight arm.

3) A lever with a low mechanical advantage (a value less than 1) requires a large effort from the muscles to move a small load — but it can move the load quickly through a large range of movement.

4) Third class levers have a low mechanical advantage — the effort arm is shorter than the weight arm.

5) A first class lever will have a high mechanical advantage if the fulcrum is closer to the load than it is to the effort, or a low mechanical advantage if the fulcrum is closer to the effort than it is to the load.

Moving joints — you'd better lever little space...

To remember the lever classes, use '1, 2, 3, F, L, E'. The letters tell you the middle component of each lever — for first class it's the fulcrum, for second class it's the load, and for third class it's the effort. Try this Practice Question.

Q1 Draw the lever system operating at the knee when standing up straight from a squat position.   [1 mark]

Planes and Axes of Movement

It might seem a bit odd that there's a page about planes and axes in a PE book — but it'll all make sense soon. Basically, you can describe a body movement using the plane it moves in and the axis it moves around.

Movements Happen *In Planes*

1) A plane of movement is an imaginary flat surface which runs through the body.
2) Planes are used to describe the direction of a movement.
3) When you move a body part (or your whole body), it moves in a plane.
4) There are three planes of movement you need to know:

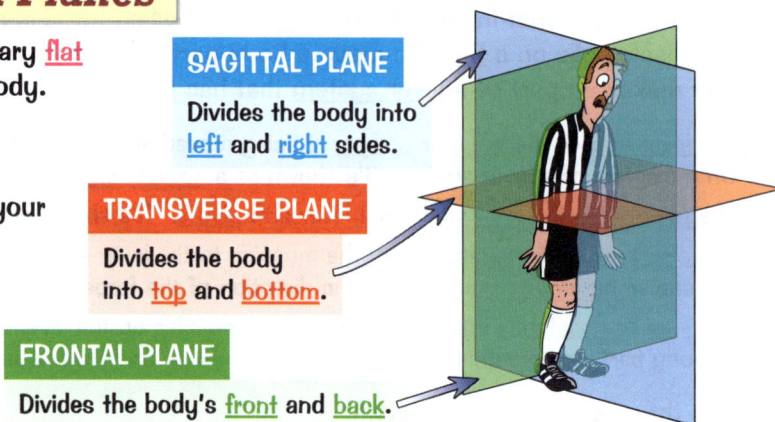

SAGITTAL PLANE
Divides the body into left and right sides.

TRANSVERSE PLANE
Divides the body into top and bottom.

FRONTAL PLANE
Divides the body's front and back.

Movements Happen *Around Axes*

1) An axis of movement (two or more are called 'axes') is an imaginary line which runs through the body.
2) When a body part (or your whole body) moves, it moves around (or 'about') an axis.
3) There are three types of axis you need to know:

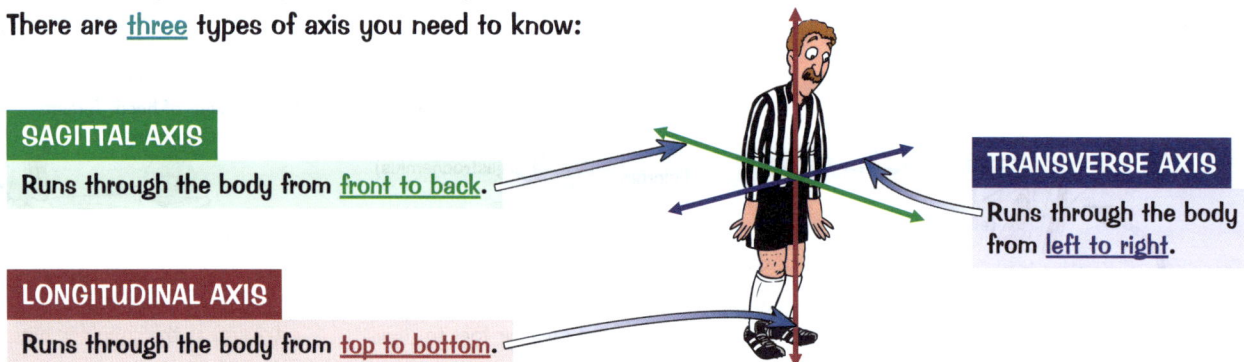

SAGITTAL AXIS
Runs through the body from front to back.

TRANSVERSE AXIS
Runs through the body from left to right.

LONGITUDINAL AXIS
Runs through the body from top to bottom.

Movements use *Different Planes* and *Axes*

Every body movement uses both a plane and an axis.
Learn the plane and axis pairs for these movement types and sporting examples.

Have a look at page 3 for more examples of the movement types.

MOVEMENT TYPE	MOVEMENT DIRECTION	PLANE	AXIS	SPORT MOVEMENTS
flexion/extension	forwards or backwards	sagittal	transverse	tucked and piked somersaults, running, forward roll
abduction/adduction	left or right	frontal	sagittal	cartwheel
rotation	clockwise or anticlockwise	transverse	longitudinal	full twist jump (trampolining), discus throw rotation, ice skating spin

These plane and axis pairs are always the same, e.g. movements that happen in the transverse plane always happen around the longitudinal axis.

Movement in planes — only when the seat belt signs are off...

The plane and axis combinations are always the same — make sure you learn the pairs for your exam. As well as the sport movements in the table, you should think of your own examples too. Have a go at this Practice Question.

Q1 State the plane and axis used during a star jump. [2 marks]

Section Two — Movement Analysis

Revision Questions for Section Two

Well, Section Two was short and sweet... Try these revision questions to make sure you took it all in.
- Try these questions and tick off each one when you get it right.
- When you've done all the questions for a topic and are completely happy with it, tick off the topic.
- The answers can all be found by looking back over pages 17 and 18.

Lever Systems (p17) ☑

1) Name the four components of a lever system.

2) State the class of each of the levers below.

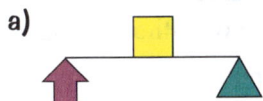

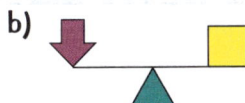

   a)   b)   c)

3) Give one example of a first class lever in the body.

4) Which class of lever is used in the foot when jumping?

5) Which lever class is used during elbow flexion?

6) What is the effort arm of a lever? What is the weight arm?

7) How do you calculate the mechanical advantage of a lever?

8) Explain what is meant if a lever system in the body has a:
   a) low mechanical advantage.
   b) high mechanical advantage.

9) Which class of lever always has a:
   a) low mechanical advantage?
   b) high mechanical advantage?

10) When does a first class lever have a high mechanical advantage?

Planes and Axes of Movement (p18) ☐

11) What is a plane of movement?

12) Which plane of movement divides:
   a) the top and bottom of the body?
   b) the left and right sides of the body?
   c) the front and back of the body?

13) What is an axis of movement?

14) Which axis runs through the body from:
   a) top to bottom?
   b) front to back?
   c) left to right?

15) Which plane and axis are used during both tucked and piked somersaults?

16) Which plane and axis are used during a cartwheel?

17) Which plane and axis are used during a full twist jump in trampolining?

18) Give a sport movement that takes place in the sagittal plane.

Components of Fitness

We'll start with telekinesis, then a bit of mind-reading... Sorry, I thought this section was Psychical Training.

Fitness *is just* One Part *of being* Healthy

1) Being healthy is more than just having a healthy body. The World Health Organisation (WHO) say:

> Health is a state of complete physical, mental and social well-being and not merely the absence of disease or infirmity.

2) Fitness is one part of good health — here's the definition:

> Fitness is the ability to meet/cope with the demands of the environment.

So, being fit means you're physically able to do whatever you want or need to do, without tiring.

3) Fitness helps with physical health, but you can have a high level of fitness without necessarily being physically healthy — e.g. some athletes overtrain and end up getting injured.

4) Mental and social well-being is also part of being healthy — being unhappy all the time isn't healthy.

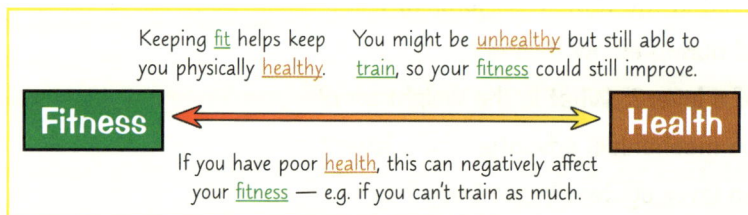

Keeping fit helps keep you physically healthy. You might be unhealthy but still able to train, so your fitness could still improve.

Fitness ⟷ **Health**

If you have poor health, this can negatively affect your fitness — e.g. if you can't train as much.

Cardiovascular Endurance — *Getting Oxygen to the* Muscles

1) Your heart and lungs work together to keep your muscles supplied with oxygen. The harder you work your muscles, the more oxygen they need.

2) So if you have a high level of cardiovascular endurance (also called aerobic power), your body is able to supply the oxygen your muscles need to do moderately intense whole-body exercise for a long time.

> CARDIOVASCULAR ENDURANCE is the ability of the heart and lungs to supply oxygen to the working muscles.

3) Most sports require good cardiovascular endurance. For example, a squash player needs to be able to keep up a fast pace all game. If a tennis player finds they are getting tired and losing points late on in a match, they will want to work on their aerobic power.

4) A high level of cardiovascular endurance is particularly important for endurance sports like cycling.

Muscular Endurance — *How* Long *'til You get* Tired

1) When you work your muscles they can get tired and start to feel heavy and weak (fatigued).

> MUSCULAR ENDURANCE is the ability to repeatedly use muscles over a long time, without getting tired.

2) Muscular endurance is really important in any physical activity where you're using the same muscles again and again — e.g. in racquet sports where you have to repeatedly swing your arm.

3) It's also dead important towards the end of any long-distance race — rowers and cyclists need muscular endurance for a strong sprint finish.

Health is wealth — you can't buy biscuits with well-being though...

Make sure you understand how health and fitness are related. Now, have a go at this Exam Practice Question...

Q1 Explain how an athlete could have a high level of fitness, but still be unhealthy. [2 marks]

Components of Fitness

Three more components of fitness on this page: strength, speed and power. Learn what they are — then make sure you learn what sports and activities each one's important in as well. Right, here we go...

Strength — the Force a Muscle can Exert

1) Strength is just how strong your muscles are.

> STRENGTH is the amount of force that a muscle or muscle group can apply against a resistance.

2) It's very important in sports where you need to lift, push or pull things using a lot of force, like weightlifting and judo.
3) Sports that require you to hold your own body weight also need a lot of strength — like the parallel bars and rings in gymnastics.
4) Strength can be broken down into different types:

- Maximal strength is the most amount of force a muscle group can create in a single movement.
- Static strength is when the muscles don't move, but still apply a force — e.g. when holding a handstand.
- Explosive strength uses a muscle's strength in a short, fast burst — it's similar to power (see below).
- Dynamic strength means using your strength to move things repeatedly, like muscular endurance (p20).

Speed — How Quickly

1) Speed is a measure of how quickly you can do something.
2) This might be a measure of how quickly you cover a distance. It could also be how quickly you can carry out a movement, e.g. how quickly you can throw a punch.
3) To work out speed, you just divide the distance covered by the time taken to do it.
4) Speed is important in lots of activities, from the obvious like a 100 m sprint, to the less obvious (like the speed a hockey player can swing their arm to whack a ball across the pitch).

> SPEED is the rate at which someone is able to move, or to cover a distance in a given amount of time.

Power Means Speed and Strength Together

> POWER is a combination of speed and strength.

> power = strength × speed

Most sports need power (also called anaerobic power) for some things. It's important for throwing, hitting, sprinting and jumping — e.g. in the long jump, both the sprint run-up and the take-off from the board require power. Here are some more examples:

I have the power.

SPORT	YOU NEED POWER TO...
Football	...shoot
Golf	...drive
Table tennis	...smash
Tennis	...serve and smash
Cricket	...bowl fast and bat

Coordination and balance (see next page) also help to make the most of power — an uncoordinated or off-balance action will not be as powerful.

Revise more I tell you — sorry, all this power's gone to my head...

Make sure you're specific about how components of fitness are used in different activities — e.g. instead of just saying 'strength helps in gymnastics' say 'strength helps the gymnast hold their body weight on the parallel bars'.

Q1 Identify **two** examples of a player using power in rugby. [2 marks]

Components of Fitness

Now it's time to look at agility, balance and coordination — just like the components of fitness on the last two pages, you need to be able to judge their importance for different activities.

Agility — Control Over Your Body's Movement

1) Agility is important in any activity where you've got to run about, changing direction all the time, like football or hockey.

2) Jumping and intercepting a pass in netball or basketball involves a high level of agility too.

> AGILITY is the ability to change body position or direction quickly and with control.

Balance — More Than Not Wobbling

Having a good sense of balance means you don't wobble or fall over easily. Here's a slightly fancier definition.

> BALANCE is the ability to keep the body's centre of mass over a base of support.

1) You can think of the mass of any object as being concentrated at just one point. This point is called the centre of mass (or centre of gravity).

2) Everything has a centre of mass — and that includes us.

3) As you change body position, the location of your centre of mass will change too.

4) Whatever activity you're doing, you need to have your centre of mass over whatever is supporting you (your base of support) to balance. If you don't, you'll fall over.

This is true whether you're moving (dynamic balance)...

...changing orientation and shape (like in dance and gymnastics)...

...or just staying still (static balance).

centre of mass

Base of support: Geoff

Base of support: arms

Show-off...

Base of support: legs

5) Balance is crucial for nearly every physical activity. Any sport that involves changing direction quickly — like football or basketball — requires good balance.

6) An action that is performed with balance is more efficient — e.g. a cyclist might work on improving their balance to increase the speed they can go round corners.

Coordination — Using Body Parts Together

> COORDINATION is the ability to use two or more parts of the body together, efficiently and accurately.

1) Hand-eye coordination is important in sports that require precision. E.g. being able to hit a ball in tennis, or shoot a bull's-eye in archery.

2) Limb coordination allows you to be able to walk, run, dance, kick, swim...

3) Coordinated movements are smooth and efficient. E.g. a runner with well coordinated arms and legs will be able to run faster than someone who is less coordinated.

4) Limb coordination is really important in sports like gymnastics or platform diving, where your performance is judged on your coordination.

Agility, Balance and Coordination — as easy as ABC...

Agility, balance and coordination all go together really. You can't be agile if you're not balanced and coordinated. Learn the definitions and how they apply to different activities, then try this Exam Practice Question.

Q1 Suggest **one** reason why a boxer needs good coordination. [2 marks]

Components of Fitness

You're nearly there now, just two more components to go. Now you have the agility, balance and coordination of a ninja, what's next? How about lightning reactions and super-flexibility? Sorry, I'm getting carried away...

Reaction Time — The Time It Takes You to React

> REACTION TIME is the time taken to move in response to a stimulus.

1) In many sports and activities, you need to have fast reactions.
2) The stimulus you respond to could be, e.g. a starter gun, a pass in football, or a serve in tennis.
3) You need fast reactions to be able to hit a ball or dodge a punch.
   It doesn't matter how fast you can move, if you don't react in time you'll miss or get hit.
4) Having fast reactions can effectively give you a head start.

Getting away quickly at the start of a sprint can mean the difference between winning and losing.

Having faster reactions in team sports can help you get away from your opponents, so you can get into better playing positions.

Flexibility — Range of Movement

1) Flexibility is to do with how far your joints move. This depends on the type of joint and the 'stretchiness' of the muscles around it.

> FLEXIBILITY is the amount of movement possible at a joint.

2) It's often forgotten about, but flexibility is dead useful for any physical activity. Here's why...

He'll bend over backwards to help you, you know.

So I've heard.

• FEWER INJURIES:
  If you're flexible, you're less likely to pull or strain a muscle or stretch too far and injure yourself.

• BETTER PERFORMANCE:
  You can't do some activities without being flexible — e.g. doing the splits in gymnastics.
  Flexibility makes you more efficient in other sports so you use less energy — e.g. swimmers with better flexibility can move their arms further around their shoulders. This makes their strokes longer and smoother.

• BETTER POSTURE:
  Bad posture can impair breathing and damage your spine.
  More flexibility means a better posture and fewer aches and pains.

Some Components are More Important than Others

1) To be good at any physical activity, you're going to need to have a high level of a number of different components of fitness.
2) For a particular activity, there will always be some components of fitness which are more important than others — e.g. in weightlifting, your strength is more important than your reaction time.
3) To compare the importance of different components, think about the kinds of actions the performer does — e.g. a batsman in cricket has to react to the bowler (reaction time), hit the ball (coordination and power), and then run (speed and cardiovascular endurance).

I'd make a joke about flexibility, but it'd be a bit of a stretch...

Congratulations, you've made it. No more components of fitness to learn. You know the drill — make sure you understand what each component is and which activities it's important in. Then it's Practice Question time.

Q1 Explain what is meant by reaction time. Identify where a fast reaction time may be beneficial. [2 marks]

Fitness Testing

So, you know what the components of fitness are — now you need to know how to measure them.

Fitness Testing Helps Identify Strengths and Weaknesses

Fitness testing gives you data that you can analyse to help improve your fitness.

1) Fitness tests are designed to measure specific components of fitness. It's important you choose the right one for the specific component you're interested in — otherwise the test is meaningless.

2) You can use fitness testing to measure your level of fitness before starting a training programme. The data will show your strengths and weaknesses, so you can plan a personal exercise programme that focuses on what you need to improve.

3) The data from fitness tests can be compared with national averages (see p26).

4) You can carry out fitness tests throughout a training programme to provide variety and to monitor your progress to see whether or not the training you're doing is working. This can help to motivate you by showing you where you're improving, and can help you to set yourself new goals.

Test your Coordination, Flexibility, Reactions and Endurance...

WALL TOSS TEST — COORDINATION

Equipment needed: stopwatch, a ball and a wall.

1) This tests hand-eye coordination.

2) Start by standing 2 m away from a wall.

3) Throw a ball underarm from your right hand against the wall and catch it in your left hand — then throw it underarm from your left hand against the wall and catch it in your right hand. You repeat this for 30 seconds and count the number of catches.

4) The more successful catches you make, the better your coordination.

5) This is sometimes called the 'alternative hand throw' or 'wall throw' test.

SIT AND REACH TEST — FLEXIBILITY

Equipment needed: ruler or tape measure and a box.

1) This test measures flexibility in the back and lower hamstrings.

2) You sit on the floor with your legs straight out in front of you and a box flat against your feet.

3) You then reach as far forward as you can and an assistant measures the distance reached in centimetres — the further you can reach, the more flexible your back and hamstrings are.

4) The distance reached can be measured in different ways — usually it's how many centimetres past your toes that you manage to reach.

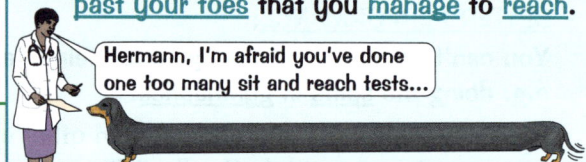

> Hermann, I'm afraid you've done one too many sit and reach tests...

RULER DROP TEST — REACTION TIME

Equipment needed: ruler.

1) Get a friend to hold a ruler vertically between your thumb and first finger. The 0 cm mark on the ruler should be in line with the top of your thumb.

2) Your friend drops the ruler — you have to try and catch it as soon as you see it drop.

3) Read off the distance the ruler fell before you managed to catch it.

4) The slower your reactions, the longer it takes you to catch the ruler, so the further up the ruler you'll catch it. This means the smaller the distance recorded, the quicker your reaction time.

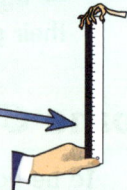

MULTI-STAGE FITNESS TEST (MSFT) — CARDIOVASCULAR ENDURANCE

BLEEP!!!

Equipment needed: tape measure, cones, multi-stage fitness test recording and some speakers.

1) A recording of a series of timed bleeps is played. You have to run 'shuttles' between two lines (marked by cones), 20 metres apart, starting on the first bleep.

2) Your foot must be on or over the next line when the next bleep sounds.

3) As it gets more difficult, the time between the bleeps gets shorter so you have to run faster.

4) If you miss a bleep, you are allowed two further bleeps to catch up. If you miss three bleeps in total, the level and number of shuttles completed are noted as your final score.

5) The higher the level and number of shuttles completed, the better your cardiovascular endurance.

Fitness Testing

Oh my, these tests just keep on coming. A load more for you to learn here, all in pretty coloured boxes...

More Tests for Components of Fitness...

30 m SPRINT TEST — SPEED

Equipment needed: stopwatch, tape measure and cones.

1) Run the 30 m (between cones) as fast as you can and record your time in seconds. The shorter the time, the quicker you are.

2) The sprint test can be done over different distances, 50 m is often used.

ONE REP MAX — MAXIMAL STRENGTH

Equipment needed: gym weight equipment.

1) The aim here is to find the heaviest weight you can lift safely using a particular muscle group. The heavier this weight, the stronger the muscle group.

2) Start with a weight you know you can lift. Once you successfully lift it, rest for a few minutes.

3) Increase the weight you attempt in small steps until you reach a weight with which you can't complete a single lift. The last weight you managed to successfully lift is your one rep max.

ILLINOIS AGILITY TEST — AGILITY

Equipment needed: stopwatch, cones and a tape measure.

1) Set out a course using cones like this.

2) Start lying face down at the start cone. When a start whistle blows, run around the course as fast as you can.

3) The course is set up so you have to constantly change direction. The shorter the time (in seconds) it takes you to complete the course, the more agile you are.

10 m
start   finish
5 m

VERTICAL JUMP TEST— POWER

Equipment needed: chalk, tape measure and a wall.

1) Put chalk on your fingertips and stand side-on to a wall.

2) Raise the arm that's nearest the wall and mark the highest point you can reach.

3) Still standing side-on to the wall, jump and mark the wall as high up as you can.

4) Measure between the marks in centimetres. The larger the distance, the more powerful your leg muscles are.

SIT-UP BLEEP TEST — MUSCULAR ENDURANCE

Equipment needed: a metronome and a non-slip surface.

1) The aim is to stick to a set pace of 20 sit-ups a minute.

2) The test is finished either when you fail to do a full sit-up in time twice in a row, or if you keep going for four minutes.

3) You count how many sit-ups you complete. The more you do the better your abdominal muscular endurance.

STORK STAND TEST — BALANCE

Equipment needed: stopwatch.

1) Stand on your best leg with your other foot touching your knee and your hands on your hips.

2) Raise your heel so you're standing on your toes and time how long you can hold the position for in seconds. Wobbling is allowed, but the test finishes if your heel touches the ground, or your other foot or hands move.

3) You usually take the best of three times in seconds — the longer the time, the better your balance.

HANDGRIP DYNAMOMETER TEST — STRENGTH

Equipment needed: a dynamometer.

1) A dynamometer is a device used to measure grip strength — the strength in the hand and forearm.

2) You grip as hard as you can for about five seconds and record your reading in kilograms.

3) Usually, you do this three times and take your best score — the higher the score, the stronger your grip.

Cheat!

'Another French pancake?' — 'No ta, I'm at my one crêpe max'...

Some tests are more suitable for certain performers than others — you should think about the actions and component of fitness measured by the test. Now, time to reveal this Exam Practice Question I prepared earlier...

Q1 Justify whether the handgrip dynamometer test is a suitable test for a rock climber. [3 marks]

Fitness Testing

You need to understand that these fitness tests are not perfect. But they still give you lots of useful data.

These *Fitness Tests* have their *Limitations*

When using any of the fitness tests, you need to consider their limitations:

1) Many of the tests do not test specific sporting actions or the movements involved in an activity.

2) Fitness tests may not tell you how an athlete will actually perform under pressure in a competition.

3) Maximal tests require working at maximum effort — e.g. the one rep max test. The results of these tests will not be accurate if the performer is not motivated to work as hard as they possibly can.

4) Many tests do not involve direct measurement and submaximal tests may be used with a formula to predict the maximum performance — so results can be inaccurate.

5) For some of the tests, you might get better scores just by getting more practice at taking the test, without the relevant component of fitness improving.

Procedures must be followed correctly to make sure the tests are valid and reliable:

- If a test is valid, this means it tests the component of fitness that it's supposed to test.

- If a test is reliable, it will give the same results if it's repeated under the same conditions. So if you see an improvement in the score, it must be because the athlete is doing better at the test.

All these *Tests* give you *Data* about your *Fitness* levels

Fitness testing gives you a number — e.g. a score, a distance, a time, etc. This is data that you can analyse to assess your fitness levels and make decisions.

These numbers are quantitative data (see p61).

1) You can compare your data over time to see how your training is going — e.g. if each week you're recording a bigger distance on the vertical jump test, you know you're increasing your leg power. There's an example of comparing data over time on page 62 — go and have a peek if you like...

2) You can also compare your own performance in a fitness test with average ratings. This can tell you how you rank compared to other people in your age group or gender.

3) Each type of fitness test will have a table that you can compare your results with.

The table below shows average ratings for 16 to 19 year-olds taking the grip dynamometer test. Let's say you want to find the rating for an 18-year-old girl who scored 26 kg:

'>' means 'greater than', '<' means 'less than'.

Gender	Excellent	Good	Average	Fair	Poor
Male	> 56 kg	51-56 kg	45-50 kg	39-44 kg	< 39 kg
Female	> 36 kg	31-36 kg	25-30 kg	19-24 kg	< 19 kg

You go down to the correct gender row.

Then read along to find the range of numbers that includes her score.

Finally, go up to see which column this range is in — that gives you the rating.

So, an 18-year-old girl who scored 26 kg on the grip dynamometer test has average grip strength for her gender.

I have a new revision workout for you — number crunches...

Analysing data might be your idea of a living nightmare, but it's key to making sense of all that fitness testing. So, make sure you understand everything on this page. Then do this little Practice Question to check you've got it.

Q1 Sarah scored 5.7 seconds on the 35 m sprint test. Using the data for the 35 m sprint test on the right, which of the following is the correct rating for Sarah?

Rating	Excellent	Good	Average	Fair	Poor
Male (seconds)	<4.80	4.80-5.09	5.10-5.29	5.30-5.60	>5.60
Female (seconds)	<5.30	5.30-5.59	5.60-5.89	5.90-6.20	>6.20

A Excellent   **B** Good   **C** Average   **D** Fair   [1 mark]

Principles of Training

Training isn't about running for as long as possible, or lifting the heaviest weights you can. There's much more to it than that — you need to know how training is matched to different people.

SPORT — The Four Principles of Training

To get the most out of your training, you need to follow these four principles:

SPECIFICITY — matching training to the activity and components of fitness to be developed.

Make sure you're training using the muscles and actions you want to improve — e.g. a cyclist would be better off improving their muscular endurance on an exercise bike than a treadmill.
You should also match the intensity of your training to the activity you're training for (see p29) and to the individual needs of the performer.

PROGRESSIVE OVERLOAD — gradually increasing the amount of overload so that fitness gains occur without injury.

The only way to get fitter is to work your body harder than it normally would — this is called overload.
To overload, you can increase the frequency, intensity, or time spent training (see next page).
This needs to be a gradual process to allow your body time to adapt. If you try to do too much too quickly, you can end up getting injured.

REVERSIBILITY — any fitness improvement or body adaptation caused by training will gradually reverse and be lost when you stop training.

Unfortunately, it takes longer to gain fitness than to lose fitness.

TEDIUM — there needs to be variety in your training, otherwise it can become boring.

If you always train in exactly the same way, it'll become boring and you'll lose motivation. Variation in training helps to keep it fresh and interesting.

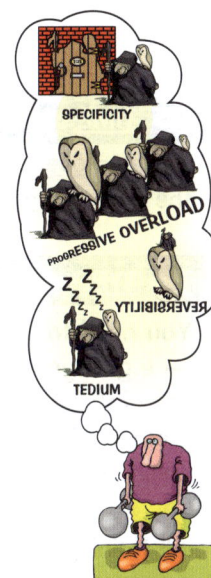

Delicious Brussels SPROTs — oh, SPORT, that makes more sense...

So that was SPORT and on the next page we have FITT — it's like no one can be bothered to write in whole, actual words anymore. Make sure you understand the concepts on this page before attempting the following EPQ...

Q1 Explain **one** way in which a rower could apply specificity to their training. [2 marks]

Principles of Training

The best training programmes aren't just thrown together — they have to be carefully planned. Part of this planning is leaving enough time for rest and recovery, so your body has time to adapt to the training.

Training Programmes can be Planned using FITT

Frequency, Intensity and Time are all part of making sure you overload while you're training.

F = FREQUENCY of training — how often you should exercise.

You can overload by increasing how often you exercise, e.g. gradually increasing the number of training sessions. You need to make sure you leave enough time between sessions to recover though (see below).

This is too intense...

I = INTENSITY of training — how hard you should exercise.

You can overload by gradually increasing the intensity of your exercise — e.g. lifting heavier weights. How intensely you train depends on the type of fitness you want to improve (see next page) and your level of fitness — someone who hasn't trained for a while should start at a low intensity and gradually increase.

I've been hula-hooping for fifty years.

T = TIME spent training — how long you should exercise for.

You can overload by gradually increasing the time you spend on a certain exercise or by increasing the overall time spent exercising — e.g. making training sessions five minutes longer each week.

T = TYPE of training — what exercises and methods of training you should use.

You need to match the type of exercise and method of training to what it is you're training for — e.g. if you want to improve cardiovascular endurance, you need to do exercise that uses lots of muscles, like running or cycling, and you should select an appropriate method of training, e.g. continuous training (see p30). Varying types of exercise also helps stop training becoming boring and reduces stress on tissues and joints.

All training programmes need to be constantly monitored to make sure that the activities are still producing overload. As you get fitter your programme will need to change to keep improving your fitness.

Your Body Adapts During Rest and Recovery

1) Training makes your body change to cope with the increased exercise. This means you get fitter.

2) These adaptations take place during rest and recovery, so it's vital you allow enough time between training sessions for the body to adapt.

3) It's also important that you allow enough recovery time between workouts to avoid over training. Over training is when you don't rest enough — it can cause injury by not giving your body enough time to recover from the last training session and repair any damage.

4) When you're training, you need to balance your recovery time with the effects of reversibility.

5) If you rest for too long, you'll lose most of the benefits of having done the training in the first place. If you don't rest enough, you could injure yourself through over training.

6) If you get injured, not only have you got to wait for your injury to heal, but thanks to reversibility your fitness will start to decrease while you do. It doesn't seem fair really...

I think I might have overdone it.

Someone's been really creative with these acronyms...

Want to be fit? Use **FITT** — **F**requency, **I**ntensity, **T**ime and **T**ype. And remember that recovery time is part of training too, because your body needs time to adapt and repair itself. Now, time for another Practice Question...

Q1   Identify **one** consequence of not having sufficient rest between training sessions.   [1 mark]

Training Target Zones

To improve aerobic or anaerobic fitness, you need to be training at the right intensity. To work this out, you have to do some calculations based on your heart rate. Don't skip a beat and read on to find out more...

Heart Rate — Heartbeats per Minute

1) Your heart rate is the number of times your heart beats per minute (bpm).
2) When you exercise, your heart rate increases to increase the blood and oxygen supply to your muscles. The harder you work, the more your heart rate will increase.
3) You can find your theoretical maximum heart rate (MHR) by doing:

$$\text{MHR} = 220 - \text{Age}$$

4) And you can use this value to work out how hard you should work to improve your fitness.

See pages 13-14 for more on how exercise affects your heart rate.

Get your Heart Rate in the Target Zone

1) To improve your aerobic or anaerobic fitness, you have to exercise at the right intensity.

Aerobic activity is 'with oxygen' and anaerobic activity is 'without oxygen' — see page 11 for more.

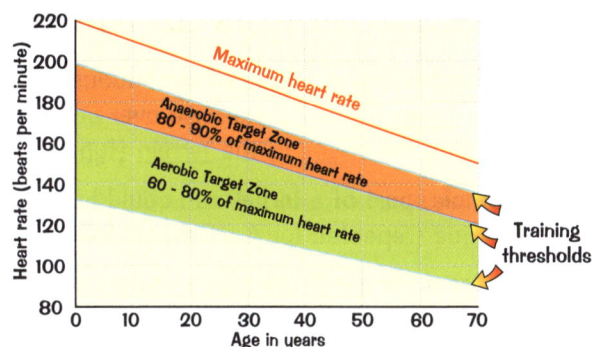

2) You can do this by making sure that your heart rate is in a target zone — there are different target zones for aerobic and anaerobic training:

AEROBIC TARGET ZONE — 60%-80% of maximum heart rate.

ANAEROBIC TARGET ZONE — 80%-90% of maximum heart rate.

3) The boundaries of the training zones are called training thresholds. If you're a beginner, you should train nearer the lower threshold. Serious athletes train close to the upper threshold.

Maximum heart rate

Anaerobic Target Zone 80 - 90% of maximum heart rate

Aerobic Target Zone 60 - 80% of maximum heart rate

Training thresholds

Heart rate (beats per minute) — Age in years

Calculating Target Zones — Example

Let's say you want to work out the aerobic target zone for a 20-year-old:

1) First, you calculate their maximum heart rate by subtracting their age from 220 — that's $220 - 20 = 200$.
2) Next you find the thresholds. Because you're calculating the aerobic target zone, the lower threshold is 60% of the maximum heart rate — that's $200 \times 0.6 = 120$. The upper threshold is 80% of the maximum heart rate — so $200 \times 0.8 = 160$.
3) So the target zone for aerobic training is between 120 and 160 beats per minute.

For the anaerobic thresholds, you'd use 0.8 and 0.9.

Your Training Intensity Should Suit Your Activity

1) If you want to be good at an aerobic activity, like long-distance running, then you should do a lot of aerobic activity as part of your training. It improves your cardiovascular system.
2) Anaerobic training helps your muscles put up with lactic acid. They also get better at getting rid of it. For anaerobic activity like sprinting, you need to do anaerobic training.
3) In many team sports, like lacrosse, you need to be able to move about continuously (aerobic), as well as needing to have spurts of fast movement (anaerobic). You should have a mix of aerobic and anaerobic activities in your training for these.

Aerobike training

I do intense training — I'm learning to juggle...

Make sure you know the percentages that go with aerobic and anaerobic target zones. Keep practising working out different target zones — the more you do it now, the easier it'll be in the exam. Speaking of practice...

Q1 Calculate the lower threshold of the anaerobic training zone for a 35-year-old. [3 marks]

Training Methods

Next up, training methods. Remember, you have to match the type of training with what you are training for.

Continuous Training Means No Resting

1) Continuous training involves exercising at a steady, constant rate — doing aerobic activities like running or cycling for at least 20 minutes with no breaks. This is also known as steady-state training.

2) It improves cardiovascular endurance and muscular endurance.

3) It usually means exercising so that your heart rate is in your aerobic training zone (see p29). This means it's good training for aerobic activities like long-distance running.

4) Overload is achieved by increasing the duration, distance, speed or frequency.

ADVANTAGES:
- It's easy to do — going for a run doesn't require specialist equipment.
- Not resting helps prepare for sports where you have to play for long periods of time without a break.

After six years of continuous training, surely I deserve a rest...

DISADVANTAGES:
- It doesn't improve anaerobic fitness.
- It can become boring doing one exercise at a constant rate.
- It can lead to injury due to repeated use of the same joints / muscles.

Fartlek Training is all about Changes of Speed

1) Fartlek training is a type of continuous training, but it involves changes in the intensity of the exercise over different intervals — e.g. by changing the speed or the terrain (type or steepness of the ground).

For example, part of a fartlek run could be to sprint for 10 seconds, then jog for 20 seconds (repeated for 4 minutes), followed by running uphill for 2 minutes.

2) It's great for cardiovascular endurance and muscular endurance and also helps to improve speed.

3) You can include a mix of aerobic and anaerobic activity, so it's good training for sports that need different paces, like hockey and rugby.

4) Overload is achieved by increasing the times or speeds of each bit, or the terrain difficulty (e.g. running uphill).

ADVANTAGE:
- It's very adaptable, so you can easily tailor training to suit different sports and different levels of fitness.

DISADVANTAGE:
- Frequent changes to intensity can mean that training lacks structure — this makes it easy to skip the hard bits and tough to monitor progress.

Interval Training uses Fixed Patterns of Exercise

1) Interval training uses fixed patterns of periods of high-intensity exercise and either low-intensity exercise or rest. It has a strict structure. For high-intensity interval training (HIIT) you use maximum effort for the high-intensity bits, and an active, low-intensity rest period.

2) By combining high- and low-intensity work, interval training allows you to improve both cardiovascular endurance and anaerobic fitness. The high-intensity periods can also improve speed.

3) It's great training for sports where you have to move continuously (aerobic), then have sudden spurts of fast movement (anaerobic) — like rugby or water polo.

4) To overload you have to increase the proportion of time spent on the high-intensity exercise, or the intensity — e.g. run faster.

ADVANTAGE:
- It's easily adapted to improve aerobic or anaerobic fitness by changing the intensity and length of work and recovery periods.

DISADVANTAGES:
- Interval training is exhausting. This can make it difficult to carry on pushing yourself.
- Risk of injury due to high intensity.

Nige's interval training: run for 1 minute, bathe for 30 minutes, and repeat...

Fartlek training — .... (Add your own joke.)

Once you're done admiring your own wit, there's an extended writing question with your name on it...

Q1 Evaluate the importance of continuous training for a marathon runner and a 100 m sprinter. [6 marks]

Training Methods

Weight training helps you to get stronger. Circuit training lets you do lots of different exercises in one go.

Weight/Resistance Training works on your Muscles

Weight or resistance training means using your muscles against a resistance. You can use weights, elastic ropes or your own body weight (like in a pull-up or press-up) as the resistance.

Improving your strength will also help increase your power.

1) Weight/resistance training can be used to develop both strength and muscular endurance.

2) It's anaerobic training, so is good for improving performance in anaerobic activities like sprinting.

3) Increasing strength/power means you can hit or kick something harder (hockey, football), throw further (javelin, discus), sprint faster, out-muscle opposition (judo), etc.

You can train by contracting your muscles to create movement. Each completed movement is called a 'rep' (repetition), and a group of reps is called a 'set'.

Example: BICEPS CURLS
Raise a dumbbell up to your chest and back down again.

See p25 for how to find your one rep max.

- To increase muscular endurance, you use low weight (below 70% of your one rep max) but a high number of reps — approximately three sets of 12-15 reps. To overload, gradually increase the number of reps.

- To increase strength you use high weight (above 70% of your one rep max) but a low number of reps — approximately three sets of 4-8 reps. To overload, gradually increase the weight — but decrease the reps to avoid injury.

- It's important you use the correct lifting technique to prevent injury and lift an appropriate weight to avoid over training.

ADVANTAGES:
- It's easily adapted to suit different sports — you can focus on the relevant muscles.
- Many of the exercises (press-ups, sit-ups, etc.) require little or no equipment.

DISADVANTAGES:
- It puts muscles under high stress levels, so can leave them very sore afterwards.
- If your weightlifting technique is poor, it can be dangerous. Also, some lifts require an assistant.

The assistant is called a 'spotter'.

Circuit Training Uses Loads of Different Exercises

Each circuit has between 6 and 10 'stations' in it. At each station you do a specific exercise for a set amount of time before moving on to the next station.

1) A circuit's stations can work on aerobic or anaerobic fitness — e.g. star jumps for cardiovascular endurance, tricep dips for strength, shuttle runs for speed, etc.

2) You're allowed a short rest between stations. An active rest, e.g. jogging instead of stopping exercising, will improve cardiovascular endurance.

3) Overload is achieved by doing more repetitions at each station, completing the circuit more quickly, resting less between stations, or by repeating the circuit.

ADVANTAGES:
- Because you design the circuit, you can match circuit training to an individual and any component of fitness — e.g. you can improve muscular endurance, strength, cardiovascular endurance... anything you want really.
- Also, the variety keeps the training interesting.

DISADVANTAGE:
- It takes a long time to set up and requires loads of equipment and space.

I prefer wait training myself — far less strenuous...

Make sure that you understand how weight/resistance training can help with muscular endurance and strength. For endurance do low weight, high reps. For strength do high weight, low reps. Keep saying it over and over...

Q1 Explain how an athlete can train using weights to improve their strength. [2 marks]

Training Methods

Plyometric training helps make you more powerful. High-altitude training improves your cardiovascular endurance for a short amount of time. Pretty intense stuff.

Plyometric Training Improves Power

Loads of sports require explosive strength and power (see p21), e.g. for fast starts in sprinting, or sports where you need to jump high, like basketball or volleyball. You can train muscular power using plyometrics.

1) When muscles 'contract' to give movement, they either shorten (concentric contraction) or lengthen (eccentric contraction) — see p5.

2) If a muscle lengthens just before it shortens, it can help to generate power. When a muscle gets stretched and lengthens, extra energy is stored in the muscle (like storing energy in an elastic band by stretching it). This extra energy means the muscle can generate a greater force when it shortens.

3) The extra energy doesn't last very long though. So, the quicker your muscles can move between the lengthening and shortening phases, the more powerful the movement will be.

4) Plyometric training improves the speed you can switch between the two phases, so it improves your power. It's anaerobic exercise and often involves jumping.

Depth jumps are a form of plyometric training. They improve the power of your quadriceps and increase how high you can jump. You drop off a box then quickly jump into the air. The first stage lengthens your quadriceps as you land and squat, the second stage shortens them as you jump.

ADVANTAGE:
• It's the only form of training that directly improves your power.

DISADVANTAGE:
• It's very demanding on the muscles used — you need to be very fit to do it, otherwise you'll get injured.

High-Altitude Training Improves Cardiovascular Endurance

1) At high altitude the air pressure is lower. This means you take in less oxygen with each breath.

2) Your body adapts to this by creating more red blood cells, so enough oxygen can still be supplied to the muscles and organs.

Land at high altitude is a long way above sea level.

3) Some athletes take advantage of this by training at high altitude to increase their red blood cell count. This gives them an advantage when they compete at a lower altitude.

4) More red blood cells means a better oxygen supply to the muscles, so it increases a performer's cardiovascular endurance and muscular endurance. This means it suits endurance athletes.

5) Training at high altitude makes it harder to reach the same intensity levels as you could training at a low altitude, so it's not well suited for anaerobic training.

6) The effects of altitude training only last for a few weeks. Once the athlete returns to a lower altitude, the body doesn't need to create extra red blood cells any more.

ADVANTAGE:
• It improves cardiovascular and muscular endurance, which helps endurance athletes perform better.

DISADVANTAGES:
• The effects only last for a short time.
• It can be very expensive to transport athletes to mountainous regions.
• While at high altitude, you can get altitude sickness. This could mean you lose valuable training time recovering.

Altitude training — it's not going to help your fear of heights...

Both the training methods covered on this page are a bit tricky — take your time and make sure you understand what components of fitness they help with, and what type of performer uses them. Time for a Practice Question...

Q1 Justify why a basketball player would train using plyometrics. [3 marks]

Training Methods

Right, last page of training methods. Make sure you understand how the different training methods can be applied to different sports. Training methods also differ in and out of competition season...

Static Stretching can be used to Improve Flexibility

This is an isometric contraction (see p5).

1) Static stretching is done by gradually stretching a muscle and then holding the position.
2) You hold the stretch at the point where you feel mild discomfort — stretching shouldn't hurt.
3) It's best to do static stretching after a workout, when the muscles are warm.
To improve flexibility, you should hold the stretches for 30 seconds.
4) To avoid injury you should always stretch gradually. This avoids overstretching the muscle.
5) Static stretching can either be active or passive:
   * In an ACTIVE static stretch, you use your own muscles to hold the stretch position.
   * In a PASSIVE static stretch, you use someone else or a piece of equipment to help you hold the stretch.

Stretching? No, I always sit like this.

ADVANTAGES:
* It improves flexibility, which can improve athletic performance.
* Almost everyone can do static stretching, even with little previous training.
* It increases the range of movement at a joint.

DISADVANTAGES:
* Poor technique can lead to overstretching and injury.
* It is only effective for stretching certain muscle groups.

Using any of the training methods covered on the last four pages over a period of time has long-term effects on the body's systems. These changes have a positive effect on both your health and performance in physical activity and sport. Make sure you know some examples of sports for which the different training methods are useful.

Training needs to be Planned Around when you Compete

Most sportspeople don't compete all year round, so they change their training programmes depending on whether it's before, during or after the competition season:

1) Pre-season (preparation) — a performer makes sure they're ready for the competitive season. The focus is on general fitness and developing the specific components of fitness and skills they need to compete. E.g. weight training is used to build up strength.

2) Competition / playing season (peak) — the performer should be at the peak of their fitness and ability. The focus is on maintaining their current level of fitness, and continuing to develop specific skills to improve their performance. If fitness training is stopped, fitness levels will drop (see reversibility, p27). However, too much training should be avoided so the performer doesn't become fatigued.

3) Post-season (transition) — once the competition season is over, the performer needs to rest and relax to allow their body to recover. Light aerobic training is done to maintain general fitness — e.g. swimming and cycling.

I'm stretching myself thin to find a good pun here...

That's it — you've made it to the end of training methods, phew. Remember that games players will still need to practise skills and actions that are specific to their sport, as well as improving relevant components of fitness.

Q1 Outline **one** training method a high jumper might use in pre-season. Justify your answer.   [3 marks]

Preventing Injuries

With any physical activity there's always a <u>risk</u> of <u>injury</u>. You need to know how to make it as <u>safe as possible</u>. After all, injury might <u>prevent</u> you from playing sport and, of course, <u>revising</u>...

To Avoid Injury do These Things...

WARM UP
- See the next page for how to <u>warm up</u> properly...

MAINTAIN HYDRATION
- <u>Drink plenty</u> of water to <u>replace</u> the water lost while <u>exercising</u>. This <u>stops</u> you becoming <u>dehydrated</u> (see p58).

USE TAPING AND BRACING
- You can use special <u>tape</u> or an elastic <u>brace</u> to <u>support joints</u>.
- This restricts the <u>range of movement</u> at a joint, which helps to <u>prevent damage to ligaments</u>.
- It's important that this is done for joints that have been <u>recently injured</u>, to help <u>avoid another injury</u>.

USE THE CORRECT CLOTHING/EQUIPMENT
- Make sure you're not wearing anything that could get caught (e.g. jewellery, watches).
- Wear suitable <u>footwear</u> — e.g. wearing studded football boots or spiked running shoes can make you less likely to slip and injure yourself.
- Use <u>protective clothing</u>/<u>equipment</u> where appropriate — e.g. gumshields, cycling helmets.

STRUCTURE TRAINING CORRECTLY
- Apply the <u>Principles of Training</u> (see p27-28).
- This means <u>planning</u> your training <u>correctly</u> — you need to avoid <u>over training</u> and allow enough time for rest and recovery, otherwise you can get <u>overuse injuries</u>. Also, make sure the <u>intensity</u> of exercise matches your level of fitness.

USE THE CORRECT TECHNIQUE
- Make sure that you use the <u>correct technique</u> — e.g. lifting weights properly, stretching without <u>bouncing</u> or <u>overstretching</u>.
- Also, make sure that you use the right technique for <u>moving</u> and <u>carrying</u> equipment.

What you do After you Exercise is Important too...

COOL DOWN
- See next page for how to <u>cool down</u>...

EAT AND REHYDRATE
- Exercising will have <u>used up</u> a lot of the <u>energy</u> stored in your body. You need to <u>replenish</u> this energy, e.g. by eating <u>carbohydrates</u> (see p57).
- You'll also need to drink plenty of water to <u>rehydrate</u> (see p58).

LEAVE ENOUGH RECOVERY TIME
- You need to leave <u>enough time</u> for your body to <u>repair</u> and <u>rebuild</u> after exercise. If you don't you could end up <u>over training</u> (see p28).

ICE BATHS/MASSAGE
- Some athletes will take <u>ice baths</u> or get sports <u>massages</u> following exercise. These may help to prevent <u>delayed onset of muscle soreness (DOMS)</u>.

Arrrrghhhhhhghghghghghhhh — I thought you said 'A nice bath'...

You need to be able to apply these ways of preventing injury to different activities, so think about the actions involved and also where the activity takes place. Now, time for an Exam Practice Question to check you've got it.

Q1   Explain how a rugby player could reduce the chance of getting injured during a match.   [3 marks]

Preventing Injuries

Warming up before exercise and cooling down afterwards are vital — they have tons of benefits.
So keep your excitement at a gentle simmer while you learn all about them...

Before Exercise you should always Warm Up...

A warm-up gets your body ready for exercise by gradually increasing your work rate. It should involve:

1) **RAISING YOUR PULSE** — light exercise increases your heart rate and gets blood flowing to the muscles.
   - This raises your body temperature and warms up muscles, ligaments and tendons so they can move more freely and are less likely to get injured. Warmer muscles can also contract more quickly.
   - It also helps to ease your body into exercising by gradually increasing the exercise intensity, and it increases the oxygen supply to the muscles.

2) **STRETCHING AND MOBILITY EXERCISES** — this increases flexibility at your joints. It should focus on the muscles and movements you will use in the activity — e.g. shoulder circles before playing tennis.
   - This helps increase the range of movement of your muscles and joints, which will help you perform better and avoid injury.

3) **PRACTICE ACTIONS** — e.g. practice shots in netball, throwing and catching in rounders, etc.
   - This prepares the muscles that will be used in the activity, so they perform better.
   - It also helps with your mental preparation, as it focuses you on the activity and gets you "in the zone".
   You could also use mental preparation techniques so you're calm, confident and focused (see page 41).

That doesn't count

...And Afterwards you should Cool Down

A cool-down gets your body back to normal after exercise by gradually decreasing the intensity of work to control your return to resting levels. It should involve:

1) **GRADUALLY REDUCING INTENSITY** — gentle exercise like jogging to keep the heart and lungs working harder than normal. You should gradually reduce the intensity of this exercise so that your heart rate, breathing rate and body temperature decrease gradually.
   - This means you can continue taking in more oxygen to help get rid of the lactic acid and other waste products in your muscles (repaying the oxygen debt — see p12). It also helps you to remove the extra carbon dioxide in your blood.
   - It keeps the blood flowing back from the muscles, so stops blood pooling in the legs and arms — blood pooling can cause dizziness and even fainting.

2) **STRETCHING** the muscles that have been used in the activity to speed up recovery and improve flexibility.
   - Static stretching (see p33) while the muscles are warm helps to improve flexibility.
   - It may also help to prevent delayed onset of muscle soreness (DOMS).

I followed that exact warm-up routine before my GCSE exams...

Warming up is especially important for more intense, anaerobic activities, where it's easy to get an injury.
Make sure you learn what warm-up and cool-downs should involve, then try this Exam Practice Question.

Q1 Evaluate the importance of a pre-match warm-up in helping a hockey player to avoid injury.   [9 marks]

Section Three — Physical Training

Revision Questions for Section Three

So, it turns out there's more to <u>physical training</u> than montages, slow motion and cheesy power ballads...

- Try these questions and <u>tick off each one</u> when you <u>get it right</u>.
- When you've done <u>all the questions</u> for a topic and are <u>completely happy</u> with it, tick off the topic.
- The answers can all be found by <u>looking back over pages 20 to 35</u>.

Components of Fitness (p20-23) ☑

1) Write a definition of health.
2) Write a definition of fitness.
3) Give two ways that exercise can help keep you healthy.
4) What is cardiovascular endurance?
5) Give an example of a sport where muscular endurance is important.
6) What is power? Give an example of when power would be needed in golf.
7) Describe coordination. How does having good coordination help a sprinter?
8) Define flexibility. Give one benefit of increased flexibility for an athlete.

Fitness Testing (p24-26) ☐

9) Describe the multi-stage fitness test. Which component of fitness does it measure?
10) Outline a fitness test that measures: a) speed, b) power, c) muscular endurance, d) agility.
11) Which component of fitness does the sit and reach test measure? What units are the results in?
12) What is meant by a reliable fitness test?

Principles of Training & Training Target Zones (p27-29) ☐

13) Name four important principles of training.
14) Give three ways that overload can be achieved in training.
15) Why is rest and recovery a vital part of training?
16) Describe how to calculate your aerobic target zone.

Training Methods (p30-33) ☑

17) Does continuous training improve anaerobic fitness?
18) Describe the fartlek training method. Give an advantage and a disadvantage of it.
19) How is overload achieved in circuit training?
20) Which component of fitness does plyometric training improve?
21) How does high-altitude training work?
22) Give an advantage and a disadvantage of static stretching.
23) Describe common differences in pre-season and playing season training programmes.

Preventing Injuries (p34-35) ☐

24) How can taping and bracing prevent injury?
25) Why is it important to use the correct clothing and equipment when playing sport?
26) What three things should be included in a warm-up?
27) Why is gentle exercise an important part of a cool down?
28) Which part of a cool down can help to prevent delayed onset of muscle soreness (DOMS)?

Learning Skills

This page is all about the different types of skill — so buckle up for plenty of thrilling definitions.

A *Skill* is Something You *Learn*

1) Skill is a word we use all the time. Here's what it means in PE:

> A SKILL is a learned action to bring about the result you want with certainty and minimum effort.

2) So a skill is something you've got to learn. You can't be born with a skill, although you might learn it more easily than other people. How easily you learn a skill is based on your ability:

> ABILITY is a person's set of traits that control their potential to learn a skill.

3) In netball, shooting is a skill because it's a learned action to help a player score goals. There are lots of inherited traits that determine a player's ability to become successful at shooting — e.g. composure to stay calm under pressure or balance to keep stable.

There are *Different Types* of *Skill*

1) There are four different skill classifications that you need to know about:

BASIC VS COMPLEX SKILLS

- A basic skill (or 'simple' skill) doesn't need much thought or decision-making to do, e.g. running.
- A complex skill needs lots of thought or decision-making to do, e.g. an overhead kick in football.

OPEN VS CLOSED SKILLS

- An open skill is performed in a changing environment, where a performer has to react and adapt to external factors. E.g. during a football tackle, you need to adapt to things such as the position of other players on the pitch.
- A closed skill is always performed in the same predictable environment — it's not affected by external factors. Often the skill involves the same action each time — e.g. when breaking off in snooker, the conditions and movement are always the same.

SELF- VS EXTERNALLY-PACED SKILLS

- A self-paced skill is controlled by the performer — they decide when and how quickly it's done.
- An externally-paced skill is affected by external factors, which control when it starts and how quickly it's done. E.g. an opponent's actions in football might determine when a pass is played and the speed it's played at.

GROSS VS FINE SKILLS

- A gross skill involves powerful movements performed by large muscle groups, e.g. the long jump.
- A fine skill uses smaller muscle groups to carry out precise movements that require accuracy and coordination, e.g. throwing a dart.

2) Many skills come somewhere in between these classifications. You can show this by putting skills on a 'continuum' (or 'scale') with one category on each end.

3) For example, you can compare the "openness" of skills by putting them on a scale like this one:

4) You can also put sport skills on a scale using the other skill classifications, e.g. a scale from basic to complex skills.

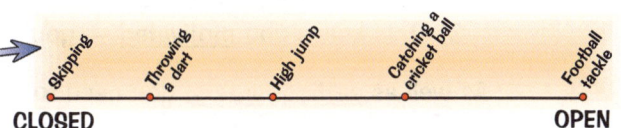

CLOSED — Skipping, Throwing a dart, High jump, Catching a cricket ball, Football tackle — OPEN

Hold the door for people behind you...

...it's a key open skill to learn. But first check you know all the skill classifications and do this Practice Question...

Q1   Justify why catching a cricket ball could be classified as an open and gross skill.   [2 marks]

Goal Setting

Setting goals and targets can often seem a bit of a hassle. But if you put the effort in and set them properly, not only do you have something to aim for, but reaching your targets can make you feel ace.

Goal Setting can Help you Train

1) Goal setting means setting targets that you want to reach so you can improve your performance.

2) Goal setting helps training by giving you something to aim for, which motivates you to work hard. Also, reaching a goal can boost your confidence and help your emotional well-being (see p55).

3) You can set yourself a performance goal, an outcome goal, or a combination of both:

   PERFORMANCE GOALS — these are based on improving your own personal performance.
   OUTCOME GOALS — these are focused on performing better than other people, e.g. winning.

4) Most of the time, it's better to set performance goals — especially if you're a beginner. Winning might be an unrealistic goal if you're new to a sport, and it can be demotivating if you lose.

5) Also, you can't usually control the result of an outcome goal, as it will depend on how well other people perform.

You need to be able to suggest suitable goals for performers of different sports and abilities.

Goal Setting Should be SMART

When you're setting targets make sure they're SMART.

S → SPECIFIC: Say exactly what you want to achieve.

1) You need to have a specific target and outline exactly what you need to do to achieve it.

2) This makes sure you're focused on your goal.

3) E.g. 'My goal is to swim 1000 m continuously'.

Goals should target specific sporting skills, movements or muscles used by the performer.

M → MEASURABLE: Goals need to be measurable.

1) This is so you can see how much you've progressed towards your goal over time — so you stay motivated to train.

2) E.g. 'My goal is to run 100 m in under 12 seconds'.

A → ACCEPTED: Goals should be decided by everyone involved — e.g. a performer and coach. The other people involved can make sure the target is set at the right level of difficulty and can motivate the performer to stay focused on it.

R → REALISTIC: Set targets you can realistically reach.

1) This means making sure you have everything you need to be able to fulfil your target.

2) That could mean being physically able to do something, or having enough resources (time, money, facilities...) to be able to reach your target.

3) This is so you stay determined during training — if it's not realistic, you could be put off.

T → TIME-BOUND: Set a deadline for reaching your goal.

1) You need a time limit to make sure your target is measurable.

2) Meeting short-term target deadlines keeps you on course to reach your long-term goals in time.

3) This keeps you motivated — you'll want to train to achieve your goal in time for your deadline.

As well as setting targets, you need to make sure you review them regularly. This is so you can see how much you've progressed towards your goal and what else you need to do to achieve it.

Goal setting — jumpers for goal posts...

Make sure you know what SMART stands for and how it can improve performance. Now try a Practice Question...

Q1 An athlete sets herself a goal to increase her running speed in six weeks.
State **one** principle of SMART goal setting that this goal does not apply. Explain your answer.   [2 marks]

Guidance and Feedback

To learn or improve a skill, you might need some guidance and feedback to help you.

Guidance — How to Perform or Develop a Skill

There are lots of different types of guidance a coach or trainer can give:

Have a look at p37 for definitions of the different skill types.

1) **VERBAL** — An explanation in words of how to perform a technique.

ADVANTAGES
1) Can be combined with other types of guidance.
2) Helpful for elite performers who'll understand any technical language.
3) Can give guidance during a performance. This is especially useful for improving open skills.

DISADVANTAGES
1) Less useful for teaching complex skills, which are difficult to explain.
2) Could be confusing for a beginner if it uses complicated language.

2) **VISUAL** — Visual clues to help you perform a technique. A coach could use demonstrations or videos and diagrams of a technique to show how it should be performed.

ADVANTAGES
1) Works well for beginners — they can copy the skill.
2) Can be used to teach closed skills — these often repeat the same action each time.
3) Slow motion videos can be useful to highlight small details of a skill for elite performers.

DISADVANTAGES
1) Less useful for teaching complex and open skills — they're more difficult to copy.
2) Demonstrations for beginners must be clear, concise and simple in order to be useful.

3) **MANUAL** — When the coach physically moves your body through the technique. For example, a coach might guide your arms when you're practising a golf swing.

ADVANTAGES
1) Useful for teaching beginners — they can get the "feel" of a skill before doing it on their own.
2) Helpful for teaching complex skills.

DISADVANTAGES
1) A performer could start to rely on it and not be able to perform a skill without it.
2) Difficult to use with big groups of learners.

4) **MECHANICAL** — Guidance given using sport equipment, e.g. a harness in trampolining.

ADVANTAGES
1) Useful for teaching beginners — they can feel safe while practising a new skill that might normally be dangerous, e.g. a somersault.
2) Helpful for teaching complex skills.

DISADVANTAGES
1) A learner might be unable to perform the skill without the help of the equipment.
2) Difficult to use in large groups.

Feedback — Finding Out How You Did

1) Feedback can be either intrinsic or extrinsic:

> **INTRINSIC** — you know how well you did the technique because of what it 'felt' like. This is called kinaesthetic feedback and works best for elite performers — they can judge how well they've performed.
>
> **EXTRINSIC** — someone else tells you or shows you what happened, and how to improve. This is suited to beginners — they don't have the experience or knowledge to accurately assess their own performance.

2) You can use feedback to work out your strengths and weaknesses and come up with an action plan to improve your performance.

Verbal guidance is just what it sounds like...

Make sure you know the advantages and disadvantages of these guidance types. You need to be able to decide whether a certain type is suitable for teaching a particular group a skill. Here's an Exam Practice Question to try...

Q1   Evaluate the use of verbal and manual guidance to improve a beginner's performance in golf.   [6 marks]

Using Feedback

More about feedback on this page, and how it's applied when you perform or practise a skill.

Feedback can Focus on Different Aspects of a Skill

1) The information in feedback can focus on different parts of a skill or movement. It might focus on:

- KNOWLEDGE OF PERFORMANCE — did you use the correct movements/technique? This can be extrinsic or intrinsic. This type of feedback works well for elite performers — it helps them to 'fine-tune' a skill that they can already perform.
- KNOWLEDGE OF RESULTS — what was the outcome? This is usually extrinsic and can include data, e.g. your time in a race. This is useful for beginners — they need to be told whether or not they achieved the right result.

2) Feedback could also focus on what you did well (positive feedback), or what you didn't do well and could improve (negative feedback).

3) It's better to avoid too much negative feedback with beginners — it can put them off learning the skill. Positive feedback is better — it helps them remember which parts of the movement they should repeat.

4) Negative feedback can be useful for elite performers. It can help to motivate them by setting a goal for them to aim for.

You're doing really well!

Feedback is part of the Information Processing Model

The information processing model divides the process of performing or practising skills into four stages:

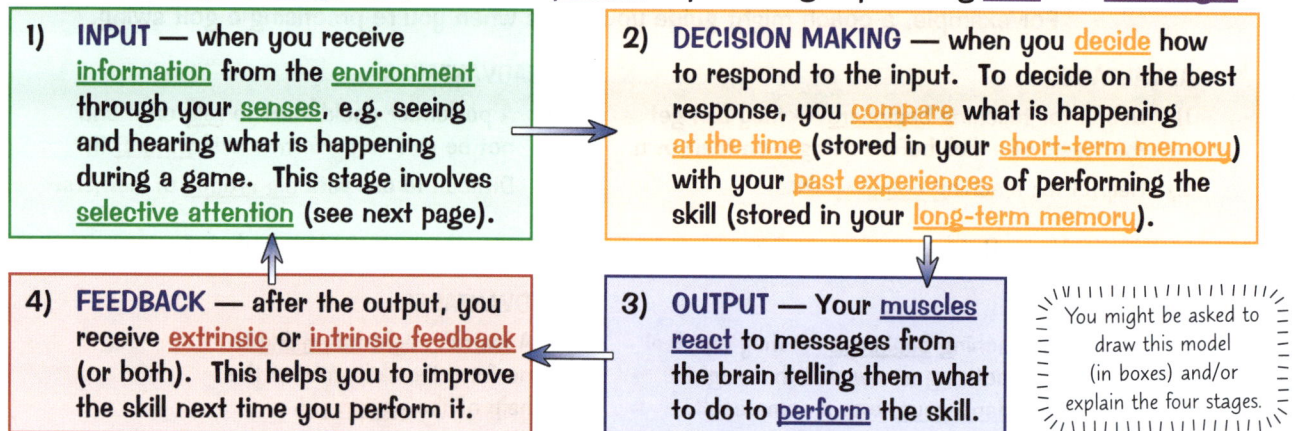

1) **INPUT** — when you receive information from the environment through your senses, e.g. seeing and hearing what is happening during a game. This stage involves selective attention (see next page).

2) **DECISION MAKING** — when you decide how to respond to the input. To decide on the best response, you compare what is happening at the time (stored in your short-term memory) with your past experiences of performing the skill (stored in your long-term memory).

4) **FEEDBACK** — after the output, you receive extrinsic or intrinsic feedback (or both). This helps you to improve the skill next time you perform it.

3) **OUTPUT** — Your muscles react to messages from the brain telling them what to do to perform the skill.

You might be asked to draw this model (in boxes) and/or explain the four stages.

You can apply this model to analyse a sports skill. For example, when taking a penalty in football:

1) **INPUT** — You'd need to pay attention to the position of the goalkeeper in front of the net and ignore distractions like noise from the crowd.

2) **DECISION MAKING** — You'd decide on the best way to perform the penalty by using what you've done in your previous practice of penalties.

3) **OUTPUT** — Your brain would send information to your muscles to tell them where to aim the shot and how powerfully to kick the ball.

4) **FEEDBACK** — You'd receive extrinsic feedback, e.g. whether or not you scored the penalty, or your coach telling you what you did right or wrong. You might also get intrinsic feedback. You could learn from this feedback how you could perform a penalty better next time.

I'd make a PE joke — but it would only get negative feedback...

Make sure you learn which types of feedback work best for different skill levels. Here's a Practice Question to try.

Q1   A snowboarding instructor praises a beginner's stance on the snowboard.
Justify the use of this feedback in helping the beginner learn to snowboard.   [3 marks]

Mental Preparation

Who'd have thought it — performing well in sport is about the mind as well as the body...

You can *Mentally Prepare* for Sport

1) Being mentally prepared is all about being able to get in the 'zone'.

2) It can help you stay focused, confident and motivated, keep control of your emotions and cope with stress so you can perform at your best.

3) There are lots of different techniques to help you mentally prepare:

> 1) MENTAL REHEARSAL is imagining the feeling in the muscles when perfectly performing a skill.
>
> 2) VISUALISATION involves imagining what an aspect of your performance should look like. It can be used as part of mental rehearsal.
>
> 3) DEEP BREATHING can help lower your heart rate (which increases when you're anxious) and make you feel more calm.
>
> 4) IMAGERY is used when you imagine being somewhere or doing something that relaxes you.
>
> 5) POSITIVE SELF-TALK/THINKING is telling yourself positive things that will motivate you or reassure you that you can perform well.
>
> 6) SELECTIVE ATTENTION is focusing on important things that will help you perform well, and ignoring things that aren't important.

Techniques 1-5 are also called 'stress management techniques' — they help lower your arousal level (see below).

4) Practising your skills during a warm-up can also help you mentally prepare (see page 35).

Your *Arousal Level* shouldn't be *Too High* or *Too Low*

1) Your arousal level is how mentally (and physically) alert you are.

2) To perform well you need to have the right arousal level. The relationship between performance and arousal can be shown on an 'inverted-U graph'.

3) The graph shows the 'inverted-U theory', which says that:

> • If your arousal level is low, then you're not very excited and you're unlikely to perform well.
>
> • At higher arousal levels, you'll be determined and ready, and should be able to perform your skills well.
>
> • If your arousal level rises too much, you become anxious and nervous. You might become tense, which can cause you to 'choke', so your performance will suffer. You might also become overaggressive.

You might be asked to draw or describe this graph in the exam.

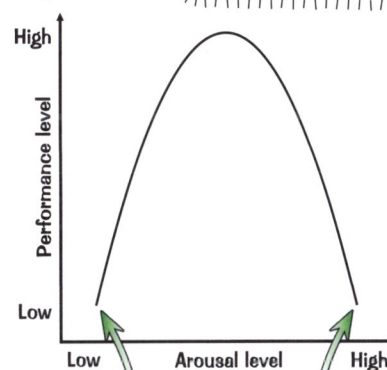

[Graph: Performance level (Low to High) on y-axis, Arousal level (Low to High) on x-axis, showing inverted-U curve]

The lowest arousal level can be called deep sleep and the highest called intense excitement.

4) The ideal arousal level varies for different skills in sport.

5) Gross skills require higher arousal levels. E.g. when tackling in football, a higher arousal level will help you commit to putting all of your effort into getting the ball. But if your arousal level is too high, you might end up hurting another player when you tackle them.

6) When performing a fine skill, you need a lower arousal level. E.g. when fielding in cricket, a lower arousal level will help you keep your hands steady to catch the ball. But your arousal level shouldn't be too low — or you won't be alert enough to move into a good position to catch the ball.

Mentally rehearse your exam for guaranteed success...

Being mentally prepared can really help your performance — so it's lucky that there are some handy techniques to help you on your way to being mentally ready for sport. Learn all about them, then try this Practice Question.

Q1   Suggest **one** reason why a football player might use mental rehearsal before taking a penalty.   [1 mark]

Emotion and Personality

This is the last page in this section now — it'll cover the types of motivation, aggression and personality.

Motivation makes you Want to Do Well

1) Motivation's about how keen you are to do something.
   It's what drives you on when things get difficult — your desire to succeed.

2) Motivation can be either intrinsic (from yourself) or extrinsic (from outside).

INTRINSIC MOTIVATION

Motivation from the enjoyment and good feelings you get from taking part in physical activity and sport, e.g. pride, high self-esteem.

EXTRINSIC MOTIVATION

Motivation through rewards from other people/ sources. This can be tangible (you can touch it, e.g. trophies, money) or intangible (you can't touch it, e.g. applause, praise from a coach).

Official CGP tug o' war champion

3) Intrinsic motivation is usually seen as the most effective — you're more likely to try hard in sport and carry on playing it in the long run if you enjoy it.

4) Extrinsic motivation can also be really effective. Rewards or praise about your performance can make you feel good about yourself — so you're more likely to want to perform well again.

5) But if you don't like a sport, extrinsic rewards on their own probably won't motivate you to try very hard at it, or play it regularly. They work better when you're already intrinsically motivated.

6) But some people think that too many extrinsic rewards can actually reduce your intrinsic motivation — so you might start to rely on extrinsic rewards to feel motivated.

Aggression can be Direct or Indirect

Aggression doesn't have to be violent — when it's used properly, it can improve your performance in sport.

1) Direct aggression involves physical contact with another person, e.g. pushing against the opposing team in a rugby scrum so you can win the ball.

2) Indirect aggression doesn't involve physical contact — a player gains an advantage by aiming the aggression at an object instead. E.g. a golfer performing a drive would use indirect aggression towards the golf ball to hit it powerfully to the green.

Introverts and Extroverts like Different Sports

The type of sport you like can be affected by your personality. You can describe someone as an introvert or an extrovert based on what their personality is like — most people are somewhere in between.

INTROVERTS are shy, quiet and thoughtful — they like being alone.
1) Introverts usually prefer sports that they can do on their own.
2) They tend to like sports where they'll need fine skills, high concentration and low arousal.
3) For example, archery, snooker and athletics are all suited to introverts.

EXTROVERTS are more sociable — they're talkative and prefer being with other people.
1) Extroverts might get bored when they're alone, so they usually prefer team sports.
2) They also tend to like fast-paced sports that need gross skills and low concentration.
3) For example, hockey, rugby and football are well-suited to extroverts.

Chocolate biscuits — an effective form of extrinsic motivation...

There's a handy way to remember what 'intrinsic' and 'extrinsic' mean. 'Intrinsic' starts with 'in', so it comes from inside you. 'Extrinsic' starts with 'ex', just like 'exit', so it comes from outside. Here's a Practice Question.

Q1   Which **one** of these is an example of tangible extrinsic motivation?
   A Praise from a teammate   **B** Wanting to succeed   **C** A medal   **D** Enjoying a sport   [1 mark]

Revision Questions for Section Four

<u>Section Four</u> has come to an end, so let's see how much you've learned.

- Try these questions and <u>tick off each one</u> when you <u>get it right</u>.
- When you've done <u>all the questions</u> for a topic and are <u>completely happy</u> with it, tick off the topic.
- The answers can all be found by <u>looking back over pages 37 to 42</u>.

<u>Learning Skills (p37)</u> ☐

1) Explain what is meant by 'skill' and 'ability'.
2) Which type of skill needs lots of thought or decision-making to perform?
3) What is the difference between an open and a closed skill?
4) Give two examples of an open skill.
5) Which type of skill has its pace controlled by the person performing it?
6) Which type of skill involves powerful movements by muscle groups?
7) Give two examples of a fine skill.

<u>Goal Setting (p38)</u> ☐

8) Why might a performer set themselves a goal?
9) What is the difference between performance and outcome goals?
    Why are performance goals usually better?
10) What do the letters in SMART stand for?
11) Explain the meaning and benefits of each element of SMART.

<u>Guidance and Feedback (p39-40)</u> ☐

12) What is guidance?
13) What is verbal guidance and why is it more suited to elite performers?
14) What is visual guidance? Why is it effective for teaching closed skills?
    Why is it less effective for teaching complex skills to beginners?
15) Give an example of manual guidance.
16) What is mechanical guidance?
17) What disadvantage do manual and mechanical guidance have in common?
18) What is feedback?
19) Explain the difference between intrinsic and extrinsic feedback.
20) What is the difference between knowledge of performance and knowledge of results?
21) Is negative feedback more useful for beginners or elite performers?
22) Describe the four stages of the information processing model.

<u>Mental Preparation, Emotion and Personality (p41-42)</u> ☐

23) What are the benefits of mentally preparing for sport?
24) Give three stress management techniques that could help lower your arousal level.
25) Explain the 'inverted-U theory' for arousal levels.
26) Why would a snooker player need a lower arousal level than a squash player?
27) Explain why intrinsic motivation is usually more effective than extrinsic motivation.
28) Explain the difference between direct and indirect aggression.
29) What type of sport do introverts usually enjoy? Give an example.

Influences on Participation

Participation means taking part in sport or other physical activities. Whether you participate in sports, and the type of sports you play, can be affected by lots of different factors...

People Influence the Activities you do

Your family and friends can have a big influence on whether you do sport, and which sports you choose.

FAMILY

1) Parents might encourage their children to take up sports, or discourage them.

2) If your parents or siblings play sport, or are interested in it, you're familiar with sport from a young age. You may also have more opportunities to take part.

FRIENDS

1) You're influenced by the attitudes of people your own age (your peers), especially your close friends...

2) For example, if all your mates play football, you're likely to play football with them. If your mates say that sport is rubbish and don't play it, you might do less sport.

ROLE MODELS

People who excel in their sport can become role models for their sport and inspire people to be like them. This encourages more people to participate in their sport.

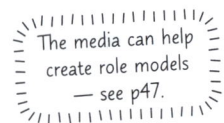

The media can help create role models — see p47.

Your Gender may Influence whether you do an Activity

Although things are getting better, there's still a real gender divide in participation. Surveys carried out by Sport England show that, overall, fewer women participate regularly in sport than men.

1) This may be because many women's events have a lower profile than men's, as they get less media coverage. This has meant that in many sports there are fewer female role models to inspire younger generations to take up the sport.

2) Less media coverage also means there is less sponsorship available for women's sport, meaning there are fewer opportunities and less money for women to do sport at a high level.

3) Gender tagging — outdated and stupid attitudes about some things being "women's activities" and others being "men's activities" — might also affect what sports you decide to take up.

4) This includes ridiculous gender stereotypes about it 'not being feminine' to get sweaty or muddy, or to play sports where you need aggression. Similarly, stereotypes about masculinity may also mean boys are expected to play more aggressive sports or are mocked for enjoying activities seen as less 'manly'.

Ethnicity and Religion can have an Effect too

1) Sometimes your religious beliefs or ethnic background can influence the physical activity you do.

E.g. many Muslim women keep their bodies covered up. This may mean they're less likely to participate in activities such as swimming because of the clothing that's expected to be worn.

2) Religious festivals and days may impact on when you can play sport. For example, some Christians won't play sport on a Sunday because it's the Sabbath, so could not join a Sunday league team.

3) Racism and racial abuse used to be a huge problem in sport. Campaigns against racism, such as the Let's Kick Racism Out Of Football campaign, have helped to raise awareness of the problem. Also, punishments for players and fans who are racist are now much more severe than they used to be.

4) Governing bodies have also tried to help create more positive role models to inspire and engage younger generations to participate.

5) Policies like the 'Rooney Rule' in American football, which says that teams must interview at least one ethnic minority candidate for any head coaching job, are also helping to create more opportunities.

That was such a good somersault — you're my roll model...

Just because these things can affect your participation in a sport doesn't mean that they should. Everyone should be able to participate in whatever sport they would like to without worrying about their ethnicity or their gender...

Q1   Explain **one** way in which your friends could affect whether or not you participate in sport.   [2 marks]

Influences on Participation

Another page of influences on participation — so many influences, so little time... Disability can influence what activities you do, and so can your job, where you live and how much money you have...

Disability can Influence how Active you are

1) Having a disability can limit the physical activities you can do. Studies show that participation rates for disabled people are lower than they are for non-disabled people.

2) The opportunities in sport and access to sporting facilities for disabled people used to be few and far between.

3) Nowadays, there are many schemes set up to give disabled people more opportunities to exercise and take part in activities within their physical limits. These schemes focus on:

- Adapting sports so that they're more accessible for disabled people — e.g. wheelchair basketball or handcycling.
- Creating new sports specifically for disabled people — like boccia (a game like bowls that can be played from a wheelchair) and goalball (a game like handball that blind people can play).
- Including disabled people in activities alongside non-disabled people. This helps to challenge stereotypes about disabled people as well as giving disabled people the opportunity to enjoy a wide range of activities.

4) Disabled sporting events are now given a lot more media coverage than they once were. The Paralympics now gets extensive media coverage, like the Olympics.

5) This media coverage is helping to change people's attitudes towards disability and sport.

6) It's also helping create many more disabled role models (like Dame Tanni Grey-Thompson and Ellie Simmonds), which encourages more disabled people to get active.

Your Socio-Economic Group can also have an Effect

Socio-economic groups are just a fancy way of grouping people based on how much money they have, where they live and the type of job they do.

- "Working class", "middle class" and "young professional" are all examples of socio-economic groups.

Recent studies seem to show that, in general, people in lower socio-economic groups are less likely to regularly take part in sport. The kinds of activities people do can also be affected by their socio-economic group.

> Yaaaar, I'm a Yuppie — a Young, Upwardly-mobile Pirate.

1) Most sports cost money. This means that some people can't afford to take part.

2) Lots of sports — like horse riding, skiing, sailing and even cycling — require specialist equipment and clothing. This can be very expensive, so could prevent people from taking part.

3) Some sports require special facilities — like ski slopes or ice rinks. If you don't live in an area with these sorts of facilities, you won't easily be able to do those sports.

4) If you don't have access to a car or good public transport to get to the facilities, this makes it a lot harder to participate. You'll be more likely to do a more accessible sport like football or basketball.

5) If you work shifts or irregular hours it can be hard to join clubs or groups that meet in the evenings or at the weekend.

6) Playing sport can also require a lot of free time. If you work long hours, or have family commitments like caring for children, you might just not have the time.

We're all under the influence...

You need to understand how all these personal factors can have an effect on participation and what sports people do. And now, treat yourself and have a pop at this Exam Practice Question...

Q1 Suggest **one** reason why having a disability might affect your participation in physical activity. [1 mark]

Influences on Participation

The final page on influences on participation — don't let it put you off getting involved...

Age can Limit the Activities you can do

1) Some sports are more popular than others with different age groups.

2) Most people aged 16-30 have loads of choice for physical activity.

3) People over 50 are more physically limited in the sports they can choose. They tend to do less strenuous activities like walking or swimming.

4) Some sports, such as weightlifting or endurance events, can potentially damage a young person's body. Competitions in these sorts of activities often have a minimum age restriction.

5) Young people often have more spare time to do sport. As people get older and have careers and families, there's less time available for playing sport.

PE in Schools can have a big effect on Participation

PE in schools plays a big role in shaping people's feelings towards sport and exercise:

1) PE classes and after-school activities are a way for students to try out lots of different sports. This allows students to become familiar with lots of activities, which might encourage regular participation. It's really important that schools offer a wide range of activities, so there's something for everyone. This will encourage more students to join in and enjoy sport:

   • Some students are put off by PE at school because they find it awkward or embarrassing.

   • Allowing students to choose what activities they would like to do, and listening to students' suggestions about improving PE, can make students more willing to take part.

   • Some students do not enjoy the competitive nature of sport, so offering non-competitive activities in PE is a good idea — e.g. fitness classes or yoga.

   • Schools can also bring in outside agencies to help with coaching and sports development.

2) Having a really good PE teacher, or sports coach at a club, can really help to inspire people too. The flip side of this is that a bad experience in PE could end up putting you off sports and exercise.

3) The facilities a school has available can limit what activities it can offer. Also, grimy old changing rooms and equipment can mean some students just aren't inspired to join in with PE at all.

You might have to Interpret Data about Participation Rates

You might be asked to analyse graphs showing participation rates for different sports and activities:

1) You may get asked to compare activities, e.g. to say which activity has increased or decreased most from one point to another.

2) The bigger the difference between these two points, the bigger the increase or decrease.

3) For example, the graph on the right shows that:

   • Participation in running increased more than football or cycling from 07/08 to 10/11.

   • Participation in football decreased more than running from 11/12 to 12/13.

Graph showing the number of English people aged 16 or over who participated at least once a week.

Number of people (millions)

An increase means going up, so the second point is higher than the first.

A decrease means going down, so the second point is lower than the first.

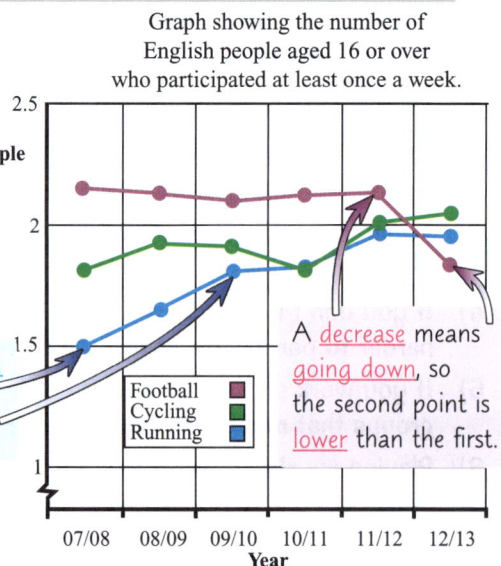

Football
Cycling
Running

Year: 07/08 08/09 09/10 10/11 11/12 12/13

Participation — you've got to be in it to win it...

All these influences work together to shape our attitude towards physical activity — make sure to get 'em learned...

Q1 Identify **two** ways that schools can encourage students to enjoy sport and physical activity. [2 marks]

Commercialisation of Sport

Lots of people are raking in cash from sport these days. This is called <u>commercialisation</u>. You need to learn how commercialisation is linked to <u>sport</u> and the <u>media</u>. Lucky for you this page has everything you need...

Commercialisation Means Making Money

1) The <u>commercialisation</u> of sport means <u>managing sport</u> in a way designed to make <u>profit</u> — mostly through <u>sponsorship</u> and the <u>media</u>.

2) <u>Sponsorship</u> is the provision of <u>money</u>, <u>equipment</u>, <u>clothing/footwear</u> or <u>facilities</u> to an individual, team or event in return for some <u>financial gain</u>.

3) The <u>media</u> (e.g. <u>television companies</u>, <u>radio broadcasters</u> and <u>newspapers</u>) pay so they can cover the sport, which means people will <u>buy</u> their <u>newspaper</u> or <u>watch</u> their <u>TV show</u>. Some companies sell sport on TV, or over the internet, as a <u>subscription package</u> too.

4) Broadcasting sports on <u>television</u> and the <u>Internet</u> means it now reaches an even larger, <u>global audience</u> — this is known as the <u>globalisation of sport</u>. This all makes sponsorship even more valuable.

5) <u>Social media</u> gives <u>fans</u> new ways to see their favourite <u>sports stars</u> and further <u>promotes</u> sponsors.

Sport, the Media and Sponsorship are all Connected

<u>Sport</u>, <u>the media</u> and <u>sponsorship</u> have grown to <u>depend</u> on one another. There are advantages and disadvantages to this relationship for the <u>sponsor</u>, the <u>sport</u>, the <u>players</u>, the <u>spectators</u> and the <u>officials</u>.

SPONSORSHIP AND SPORT

1) Sponsorship deals mean companies can associate their name with the <u>prestige</u> of successful <u>sportspeople</u> and <u>teams</u>. This is an effective form of <u>advertising</u>, which helps <u>the sponsor</u> to make more money.

2) These deals mean <u>big money</u> for sport — which can be spent on <u>development</u>, e.g. of a new stadium or facilities. This benefits the <u>players</u> and the <u>spectators</u>. This money can also pay for technology to help <u>officials</u> (see p49).

3) Sponsorship money also means <u>players</u> and <u>officials</u> can be paid good <u>wages</u>, and players can train full-time. This benefits <u>everyone</u>, because they will <u>perform</u> better.

SPONSORSHIP AND THE MEDIA

1) The more <u>media coverage</u> a sport gets, the more people <u>watch</u> it. This makes <u>sponsorship</u> more <u>valuable</u>, as it can reach a <u>larger audience</u>.

2) This increases the likelihood of sponsorship and means <u>the sport</u> and <u>players</u> can <u>demand more money</u> for their sponsorship deals.

THE MEDIA AND SPORT

1) The media <u>pay</u> for the rights to cover sporting events, which provides <u>investment</u> for <u>sports</u> to <u>develop</u> at lower levels.

2) Media coverage makes <u>more</u> people <u>aware</u> of the sport, so more people may <u>play</u> it or watch it.

3) Media coverage of <u>elite</u> players and athletes can create <u>role models</u> who <u>inspire</u> people to play.

4) This can make <u>players</u> into superstars. But the downside is that <u>players</u> are <u>hounded</u> by the media and their <u>private lives</u> are all over the news.

5) Also, the media can hold so much <u>power over</u> sport that they'll <u>change</u> things:

- The <u>number</u> of games played, or the <u>timings</u> of matches, might be changed so more matches can be shown. This risks <u>injury</u> to <u>players</u> through lack of rest, and might mean <u>spectators</u> miss a game because it's not at a convenient time.

- Also, <u>rules</u> may be changed — e.g. the <u>tiebreaker</u> set was brought into tennis to make matches shorter.

6) Being able to watch on <u>TV</u> or the <u>Internet</u>, rather than going to the game, can save <u>fans</u> money. However, fewer fans buying tickets means losses in ticket sales for <u>the sport</u> and a poorer atmosphere at the stadium for <u>spectators</u>.

7) The media's <u>analysis</u> of refereeing decisions puts <u>sports officials</u> under a lot of <u>pressure</u>.

8) Media analysis of games can also <u>educate</u> <u>spectators</u>, so they <u>understand</u> the sport better.

I don't write these jokes for the money — I do it for the love, man...

Get this commercialisation stuff memorised and the marks will flow like famous footballers' sponsorship deals.

Q1 Explain **two** ways that media interest in a sport can encourage more people to take part. [4 marks]

Commercialisation of Sport

Sponsorship can be a little complicated. You need to know that it has its downsides and that not all types of sponsor are suitable. Read on to find out about the dark side...

Sponsorship Isn't All Great

1) Sometimes, the money is only available for the top players and teams, so benefits the elite — not the sport as a whole.

2) It could all turn nasty — if an athlete gets injured, loses their form or gets a bad reputation they could lose their sponsorship deal. Bad behaviour by an athlete reflects badly on the sponsor too and could damage the company's reputation.

3) Sometimes athletes have to fulfil contracts with their sponsor — they might have to turn up at a special event or appear in a TV advert (even if they don't want to).

4) Athletes can get into trouble with their sponsor if they're spotted using another company's products.

5) If a team really needs a sponsor's money, this puts the sponsor in a position of power. This means they can influence the team's playing style or team selection.

6) In some sports where there are breaks in play, adverts will be shown. The game won't be allowed to restart until the advert break is finished, which can be quite boring for spectators in the stadium.

Why's he playing?

His Dad sponsors the team.

Some Sponsors are Inappropriate

Sponsorship brings in loads of money, but you have to be careful not to promote the wrong image, especially in youth sports:

1) Cigarette and tobacco companies aren't allowed to sponsor sports in the EU. This is because their products are harmful and unhealthy.

2) Alcoholic drinks companies are allowed to sponsor some sports, but this can be bad as it gives alcohol a false image of health. The same is true for unhealthy food companies.

3) Also, as sport is watched by children, advertising alcohol and fast food could be encouraging young people to drink or eat unhealthily.

You can Interpret Data About Commercialisation

There's lots of data to do with commercialisation of sport, so here's an example and how you can interpret it:

1) The graph on the right shows the total amount spent each year on shirt sponsorship (that's companies paying to have their logo on the front of a team's shirt) in the Premier League.

2) The graph shows that every year since 2010, spending on shirt sponsorship in the Premier League has increased (there is an "upward trend").

3) If the graph carried on past 2015, you'd expect it to keep on going upwards.

4) You can also see that the biggest increases in spending were from 2011 to 2012 and from 2014 to 2015 — shown by the line going up more steeply.

A graph showing the amount spent on shirt sponsorship in the Premier League between 2010 and 2015.

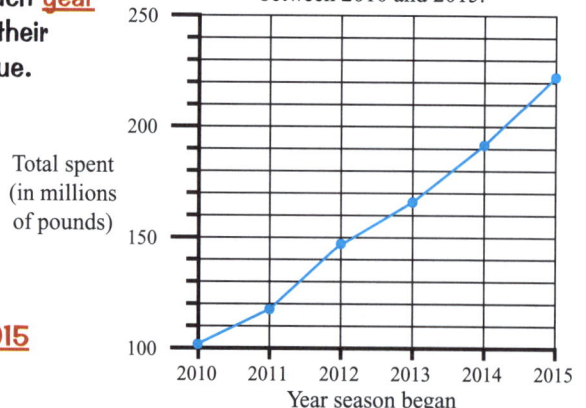

Total spent (in millions of pounds)

250

200

150

100

2010 2011 2012 2013 2014 2015

Year season began

CGP CGP CGP CGP (CGP — Official Sponsors of page 48)...

It's important that you can weigh up the pros and cons of sponsorship, especially when it comes to fast-food and alcohol companies. Have a go at this Exam Practice Question to check you've got it...

Q1 Discuss the impact on an under-12's football team of being sponsored by a fast-food company.   [4 marks]

Technology in Sport

There's loads of technology used in sport — make sure you learn all about it for the exam.

Technology can help Players to Perform Better

1) Lots of the technology used today is designed to help athletes perform better at their sports. This benefits spectators as well as performers, as new levels of sporting excellence are achieved.

2) New materials are used to make sports equipment and clothes more effective — from shoes to swimming costumes to tennis rackets. This helps players reach new levels of performance.

3) Improvements to training facilities, like all-weather pitches, mean that training doesn't have to stop for bad weather. This means more time can be spent training, so performances will improve.

4) There have also been developments to make sports safer, like better protective clothing and better playing surfaces. Also, medical technology can help athletes recover from injuries quickly and safely.

5) Video footage and 3D modelling software can be used by coaches to analyse an athlete's movement. This can be done to a very high degree of accuracy, so an athlete's technique can be fine-tuned. In events like the 100 m sprint, where winning may come down to a few milliseconds, this level of accuracy is really important.

Tony used ICT to improve his dropkick technique.

6) All this technology is expensive though. This can mean that only people with lots of money can compete at the highest level.

7) There is a worry that technology can give athletes an unfair advantage over their competitors. If sport becomes less about the abilities of the athletes and more about the technology they're using, it kind of stops being interesting for spectators.

Technology can help Officials to make Correct Decisions

Many sports now make use of technology during matches to help referees and umpires.

Out!

Hawk-Eye (tennis) — Hawk-Eye uses a set of six cameras to track and predict the path of the ball. It's used so that players can challenge the decision of whether shots are in or out.

Decision Review System (DRS) (cricket) — players are allowed to challenge an umpire's decision and have it reviewed by the third umpire, who uses various bits of technology (including Hawk-Eye) to decide whether the on-field umpire was correct or not.

Television Match Official (TMO) (rugby union) — the TMO is an extra official who watches video replays. The referee on the pitch can consult with the TMO to help them make key decisions.

Goal-line technology (football) — there are cameras pointed at each goal that are used to tell whether or not the ball has crossed the goal line.

ADVANTAGES

1) All these systems help to make the sport more fair, which benefits spectators and players by avoiding the frustration of wrong decisions.

2) They help officials to make valid and reliable decisions, even in marginal situations. This lessens the pressure on them.

3) The DRS in cricket has shown that the umpires are right most of the time. This has led to increased respect for umpires.

4) Sponsors can use the breaks in play that some of these technologies cause to show adverts.

DISADVANTAGES

1) These systems are expensive to install, so are only used at the top end of sporting leagues.

2) The fact that things can be reviewed could undermine the authority of the officials on the pitch. This could lead to players contesting every decision the referee makes.

3) Referring to a video replay can sometimes take a long time. Some people worry that these breaks disrupt the flow of play and can also be boring for spectators.

'Owzaaaat?!'

I could be a TMO — they just sit around watching sport on TV...

Cyborg-boxing and techno-jocks — bring on the technology in sport I say. I, for one, welcome our new robot overlords... What rhymes with 'Sham Cactus Session'? That's right, Exam Practice Question. Now, hop to it...

Q1 Using sporting activities, outline the use of technology and justify the impact it can have on sport. [9 marks]

Sporting Behaviour

This page is about good and bad behaviour in sport. Turns out taking your ball home if you're losing isn't okay. Neither is standing in the corner sulking if the other team score. Make sure you learn the following definitions...

Sportsmanship is About Being Fair and Humble

Being a good sportsperson is more than just playing by the rules. You also have to show good 'sportsmanship' (even if you lose) and uphold the 'contract to compete'.

> Sportsmanship means playing within the rules, upholding the spirit of the game and using sports etiquette.

> The contract to compete is an agreement between competitors to comply with all the rules (both written and unwritten).

1) Good sportsmanship means no rubbing it in the opposition's face if you win. And no going off in a huff if you lose.
2) It also means observing the etiquette of an activity.

> Sporting etiquette means following the unwritten rules and conventions of the activity.

Etiquette is not a list of enforceable rules (i.e. players can't be punished for poor etiquette), but it is usually observed. Here are some examples...
- In cricket, a batsman might choose to 'walk' if they think they've been caught out — even if the umpire has ruled them not out.
- In football, players will kick the ball out of play if a member of the other team goes down injured.
- Players shake hands with officials and opponents after a match, regardless of the outcome.
- In cycling, if someone has a mechanical problem with their bike (like a puncture), the other riders will not take advantage by speeding up until the problem is fixed.

Gamesmanship is a type of Poor Behaviour

> Gamesmanship is gaining an advantage by using tactics that push the rules without breaking them.

Gamesmanship is not actually cheating — but it can come quite close. A lot of the techniques are about breaking up the flow of a game, or distracting your opponents:

1) Time-wasting in football is when players deliberately faff about. This runs down the clock and breaks up the flow of the game.
2) In tennis, some players make loud grunting or shrieking noises when they hit the ball to try and intimidate or distract their opponent.
3) In basketball, a manager might call a timeout just as the opposition win a free throw. This is to try and make them overthink the shot.

1) Gamesmanship does not normally result in punishment for the players, although if it is taken too far referees might get involved.
2) Using performance-enhancing drugs (see next page), deliberately fouling an opponent or being violent and aggressive are not gamesmanship — they all go against the moral values or laws of the sport.

Footballers ought to be gracious in defeat — they use 'em enough...

Remember that sportsmanship is all about 'being a good sport.' It's a really important part of being a team player and having a fair game. So be a sport and have a go at this Exam Practice Question...

Q1 Describe the difference between sportsmanship and gamesmanship. [2 marks]

Performance-Enhancing Drugs

Some people <u>cheat</u> by taking <u>drugs</u>. Drugs can help them <u>perform better</u>, but they can also cause serious <u>health problems</u>. You need to know the <u>positive</u> and <u>negative</u> effects of these drugs on the performer...

Performance-Enhancing Drugs can Improve Performance

1) Some performers use drugs to <u>improve</u> their performance and be more <u>successful</u> in their sport, which can lead to <u>wealth</u> and <u>fame</u>. Some performers also claim they use drugs to <u>level the playing field</u> — if other competitors use drugs, you're at a disadvantage unless you use them too.

2) The use of these drugs in sport is usually <u>banned</u>, and they can have <u>nasty side effects</u>. Being caught using these drugs can lead to <u>fines</u>, <u>disqualification</u> or lengthy <u>bans</u> for cheating.

3) Unfortunately, some performers still <u>break the rules</u> by taking them anyway — even with the <u>risks</u> to their <u>health</u> and <u>reputation</u> and to the <u>reputation</u> and <u>credibility</u> of their <u>sport</u> if they're caught. These are the drugs you need to know about:

BETA BLOCKERS

- <u>Reduce heart rate</u>, <u>muscle tension</u>, <u>blood pressure</u> and the <u>effect of adrenaline</u>. This <u>steadies shaking hands</u>, which improves <u>fine motor skills</u>.
- This <u>calming</u>, <u>relaxing</u> effect is beneficial in e.g. <u>shooting sports</u>.

But...

- They can cause <u>nausea</u>, <u>weakness</u>, <u>cramp</u> and <u>heart failure</u>.
- They're <u>banned</u> in some sports and if allowed must be <u>prescribed</u> by a <u>medical professional</u>.

DIURETICS

- Increase the amount you <u>urinate</u>, causing <u>weight loss</u> — which is beneficial if you're competing in a certain <u>weight division</u> (e.g. as in <u>boxing</u> or <u>judo</u>).

But...

- They can cause <u>cramp</u>, <u>dehydration</u>, <u>loss of salts</u>, <u>muscle weakness</u> and <u>heart damage</u>.

NARCOTIC ANALGESICS

- <u>Kill pain</u> — so injuries and fatigue, e.g. from overtraining, don't affect performance and training so much.

But...

- They're <u>addictive</u>, with unpleasant <u>withdrawal symptoms</u>.
- Feeling less pain can make an athlete train <u>too hard</u>, causing <u>overtraining</u>.
- They can lead to <u>constipation</u> and <u>low blood pressure</u>.

STIMULANTS

- Affect the <u>central nervous system</u> (the bits of your brain and spine that control your <u>reactions</u>).
- They can <u>increase mental</u> and <u>physical alertness</u>.

But...

- They can lead to <u>high blood pressure</u>, <u>heart</u> and <u>liver problems</u>, and <u>strokes</u>.
- They're <u>addictive</u>.

ANABOLIC AGENTS (STEROIDS)

- Mimic the male sex hormone <u>testosterone</u>.
- Testosterone <u>increases</u> your <u>bone</u> and <u>muscle growth</u>, so you can get bigger and stronger, but also more <u>aggressive</u>.
- Help with <u>faster</u> recovery from exercise and are commonly taken by <u>sprinters</u>.

But...

- They can cause <u>high blood pressure</u>, <u>heart disease</u> and <u>infertility</u>, and can increase the risk of developing <u>cancer</u>.
- Women may grow <u>facial</u> and <u>body hair</u>.

PEPTIDE HORMONES (EPO)

- Cause the production of other <u>hormones</u> — similar to anabolic agents.
- <u>EPO</u> (Erythropoietin) is a peptide hormone that causes the body to produce more red blood cells. This <u>increases oxygen-carrying capacity</u> and <u>endurance</u>, which benefits, e.g. <u>road racing cyclists</u>.

But...

- They can cause <u>strokes</u>, <u>heart problems</u>, <u>abnormal growth</u> and <u>diabetes</u>.

Blood Doping Increases Red Blood Cell Count

1) Blood doping increases the number of <u>red blood cells</u> in the bloodstream. This increases <u>oxygen supply</u> to the muscles and <u>improves</u> performance and endurance.

2) The increase in <u>cardiovascular endurance</u> can benefit athletes such as <u>long-distance runners</u> and <u>cyclists</u>.

3) One method of blood doping involves <u>removing</u> some blood from an athlete several weeks before a competition. The blood is <u>frozen</u>, then <u>re-injected</u> before the athlete competes.

4) Possible side effects of injecting red blood cells include <u>blood thickening</u> (viscosity), <u>infections</u>, <u>increased risk of heart attack</u> and <u>blocked blood vessels</u> (embolism).

Blood doping is banned but can be hard to test for.

This drug is anabolic, it's diabolic — why it's health blighting...

Make sure you can give examples of performers in different sports who might use these drugs.

Q1   Identify one performance-enhancing drug that an archer might use. Explain your choice.   [2 marks]

Spectator Behaviour

Big sporting events draw big crowds — this has both advantages and disadvantages. Make sure you learn what these are — I'm watching you...

You only sing when you're winning, sing when you're wiiiiinnniiiing....

Spectators create an *Atmosphere*

1) Crowds at sporting events create an atmosphere and this adds to the excitement, making the event more enjoyable for spectators and players.

2) Also, this can create a 'home-field advantage' — the 'home' team perform better because they're in familiar surroundings with more fans supporting them. This can also intimidate the opposition.

3) However, sometimes all those spectators can put pressure on the performers, who end up performing worse because they are nervous and afraid to make mistakes.

4) Having spectators at sporting events for younger people (like youth leagues in football) can put more pressure on the kids who are taking part. This can discourage children from taking up activities, so can negatively affect participation rates (see pages 44-46).

5) At big events, it takes a lot of planning and money to make sure spectators are safe. With large groups there's the chance of crowd trouble and hooliganism...

Pah, hooligans the lot of you...

Hooliganism is when fans *Become Aggressive*

Hooliganism is rowdy, aggressive and sometimes violent behaviour of fans and spectators of sport. You need to know what causes hooliganism and how it can be prevented...

CAUSES

1) Rivalries between fans. These rivalries might be built up by the press and the media so they seem even more important. This hype can cause fans to take the match too seriously.

2) Some fans might have been drinking, or even taking drugs, which can fuel aggression and violence.

3) Frustration with decisions made by officials, or just frustration with how the match is going, can lead to spectators getting angry.

4) Some people see hooliganism as a display of masculinity, or a way of fans proving themselves to be macho. Peer pressure can make people feel they have to join in. There could also be a 'gang mentality', where people feel less responsible for their actions because they're in a group.

METHODS OF PREVENTION

1) Kick-offs can be made earlier for games where it's likely there will be trouble. This leaves less time between the pubs opening and the start of the game, so fans will be less drunk during the game. Alcohol restrictions can also be brought in to control buying alcohol within the stadium.
   - However, fans often get round this by drinking more before they go to the game. Also, having earlier kick-offs can make it inconvenient for travelling fans to get to the game.

2) Making every stadium 'all-seated' so fans don't have to stand. This is safer because people are less packed together. It's also easier for stewards and police to get to troublemakers.

3) Fans can be segregated (sat in separate sections) to stop fighting inside the ground. Sometimes home and away fans enter and leave the ground at different times.
   - This doesn't help prevent violence outside of the stadium though, and it can mean it takes longer for fans to get into or out of the stadium, which is annoying for the fans.

4) The number of police and stewards at games can be increased, which boosts security in the ground. Also, video surveillance and other technology can be used to monitor crowds.
   - It can be very expensive to install all this technology and pay extra police and stewards.

5) For fans who have committed hooliganism in the past, there are banning orders and travel restrictions, e.g. confiscating passports. This means that the worst offenders aren't at games.

6) There have been lots of campaigns to educate fans about the harm that's caused by hooliganism.

Hooliganism — a silly word but a serious issue...

For the methods of preventing hooliganism, it's important you learn their drawbacks. It's Practice Question time...

Q1 State **two** reasons why hooliganism might occur at a football match. [2 marks]

Revision Questions for Section Five

That's Section Five done and dusted — now be a good sport and have a go at these revision questions.
Try these questions and tick off each one when you get it right.

- When you've done all the questions for a topic and are completely happy with it, tick off the topic.
- The answers can all be found by looking back over pages 44 to 52.

Influences on Participation (p44-46) ☑

1) Give one way that your family and friends might influence your participation in sport.
2) How can your gender influence what sports you participate in?
3) How can religious beliefs influence what sports you participate in?
4) How can the media help improve participation rates amongst the disabled?
5) What is meant by a socio-economic group?
6) Outline one way that the amount of money you have could affect your participation in sport.
7) Describe two ways that your age can limit your participation in physical activities.
8) Give one example of a sporting activity that is inappropriate for a very young person to participate in.
9) Why might school PE lessons put students off sport and exercise?

Commercialisation of Sport (p47-48) ☑

10) What does 'commercialisation' mean?
11) Give one effect of increased media coverage on a sport.
12) Give one advantage and one disadvantage of sponsorship for a sport.
13) If a sports team gets media coverage, what might happen to the value of their sponsorship deals? Give a possible reason for this happening.
14) Give one way an athlete could lose their sponsorship deal.
15) Which of these cannot sponsor an EU football team: a) a car manufacturer, b) a tobacco company?

Technology in Sport (p49) ☑

16) Outline three ways technology can help an athlete perform better.
17) Why might technology make sport less interesting for the spectators?
18) Give an advantage and a disadvantage of using technology to help officials during a match.

Sporting Behaviour and Performance-Enhancing Drugs (p50-51) ☑

19) Give a definition and an example of:
    a) Sportsmanship
    b) Gamesmanship
    c) Etiquette
20) What is meant by the 'contract to compete'?
21) Give three disadvantages of a performer taking performance-enhancing drugs.
22) Describe the positive and negative effects of: a) beta blockers, b) diuretics, c) stimulants.
23) What side effects can occur as a result of blood doping?

Spectator Behaviour (p52) ☐

24) How can the 'home-field advantage' help the home team to perform better?
25) What negative effect can spectators have on the players?
26) Give a definition of hooliganism. Name one thing that can cause hooliganism.
27) Outline three methods that can be used to prevent hooliganism.

Health, Fitness and Well-being

Regular physical activity helps you to be healthy by improving your physical, emotional and social health and well-being. First up, the obvious one — exercise helps keep you physically healthy...

If your Body Works Well, you are Physically Healthy

> See p15 for more about how exercise benefits your body systems.

1) Physical health and well-being are important parts of being healthy and happy.
2) Taking part in sport or other physical activities has loads of physical benefits.

PHYSICAL HEALTH AND WELL-BEING:

1) Your body's organs, e.g. the heart, and systems, e.g. the cardiovascular system, are working well.
2) You're not suffering from any illnesses, diseases or injuries.
3) You're strong and fit enough to easily do everyday activities.

2) These positive effects on the body reduce the risk of obesity and other long-term health problems (see below). Stronger muscles and more flexible joints can make injury less likely and improve your posture. Avoiding injury also means you can continue training.

1) By exercising you can improve components of fitness (see p20-23), which benefits your physical health:
- Aerobic exercise improves your cardiovascular endurance — your heart, blood vessels and lungs work more efficiently, so you can exercise more intensely and for longer. Your blood pressure also decreases.
- Exercise can benefit your musculo-skeletal system — muscles and bones get stronger, and joints more flexible.
- Exercise helps you to reach and maintain a healthy weight, which reduces strain on your body.

3) Physical activity makes you stronger and fitter — so everyday tasks like climbing stairs and lifting shopping are easier. This can help your emotional well-being too (see next page). It's not all good though — overtraining (see p28) can have a negative effect on your health.

> Novelty size veggies ltd.

> Now that's what I call shoplifting.

Exercise Reduces Risks to Long-Term Health

Regular physical activity can help reduce the risks of you getting certain diseases. For example:

1) Regular aerobic exercise helps prevent high blood pressure by keeping your heart strong and arteries elastic, and helping to remove cholesterol from artery walls.
2) This means blood can flow easily round the body, which reduces the risk of coronary heart disease (CHD), strokes and damage to your arteries.

> Exercise increases levels of high density lipoprotein (HDL). HDL helps to remove cholesterol from the arteries.

Regular exercise helps prevent obesity. Exercise uses up energy, meaning that your body doesn't store it as fat (see p56).

1) Diabetes is a disease that gives you a high blood sugar level.
2) Your blood sugar level is controlled by a hormone called insulin. If you have diabetes, this means you don't have enough insulin or your body's cells aren't reacting to insulin properly.
3) Regular exercise helps you to maintain a healthy weight. This makes you far less likely to get diabetes.

> Middle-aged and older adults have a far higher risk of diabetes, so exercise is a great way for them to lower that risk.

All these benefits of exercise and I'm sitting around writing jokes...

Remember that health and fitness are defined back on p20 — flick back and take a look if you need a little reminder... And now, here's an Exam Practice Question for you, because I know how much you love 'em.

Q1   Outline **two** benefits of exercise to an individual's physical health and well-being.   [2 marks]

Health, Fitness and Well-being

As well as making you into a Schwarzenegger-like picture of physical health, exercise is great for your <u>emotional</u> and <u>social</u> health. You need to be able to give examples of <u>how</u> it helps.

Emotional Health is about how you Feel

Emotional health can also be called 'mental health'.

1) Being <u>healthy</u> is more than just having a body that works well — you also have to take into account how you <u>feel</u>. Your <u>emotional health</u> and <u>well-being</u> is based on how you feel about yourself and how you respond to different situations.

2) Taking part in physical activity and sport can have <u>emotional benefits</u>:

I'm amazing...

EMOTIONAL HEALTH AND WELL-BEING:

1) You feel <u>content</u> and <u>confident</u> in yourself.
2) You are able to <u>manage</u> your <u>emotions</u> and <u>cope</u> with <u>challenges</u>.
3) You don't have too much <u>stress</u> or <u>anxiety</u>.
4) You're not suffering from any <u>mental illnesses</u>.

1) Physical activity can increase your <u>self-esteem</u> (your opinion of yourself) and <u>confidence</u> and generally make you <u>feel better about yourself</u>, e.g. if you feel you've achieved something. Seeing <u>improvements</u> in your <u>physical health</u>, e.g. losing weight or gaining strength, can improve your <u>self-image</u>.

2) <u>Competing</u> against others (or yourself) can improve your ability to <u>deal</u> with <u>pressure</u> and <u>manage emotions</u>, e.g. by giving you a controlled way to channel your aggression. It's also a great way for <u>young children</u> to learn these <u>skills</u>.

3) Doing physical activity can help <u>relieve stress</u> and <u>tension</u> by taking your <u>mind off</u> whatever's worrying you and by making you feel <u>happier</u>. This helps prevent <u>stress-related illnesses</u>.

4) When you do physical activity, <u>feel good hormones</u> (like <u>serotonin</u>) are released. An <u>increased</u> level of <u>serotonin</u> in your brain may reduce your risk of developing <u>mental illnesses</u>, like <u>depression</u>.

Stressed? Me? Don't be ridiculous.

Social Health is about how you Relate to Society

1) Your <u>social health</u> and <u>well-being</u> is about how you interact with <u>others</u> and <u>form relationships</u>.

2) There can be plenty of <u>social benefits</u> from doing physical activity and sport:

SOCIAL HEALTH AND WELL-BEING:

1) You have <u>friends</u>.
2) You believe you have some <u>worth</u> in society.
3) You have <u>food</u>, <u>clothing</u> and <u>shelter</u>.

1) Doing physical activity can help you <u>make friends</u> with people of different <u>ages</u> and <u>backgrounds</u>. For example, some elderly folk may have fewer opportunities to <u>socialise</u>, so sport can be a great way to make new friends. It's also a great way of <u>socialising</u> with your <u>current friends</u>.

2) By taking part in <u>team activities</u> like football, you have to practise <u>teamwork</u> — how to <u>cooperate</u> and <u>work with other people</u>. These skills are <u>useful</u> in all walks of life and can help you to be <u>successful</u>, which will increase your sense of <u>worth</u>. Being part of a team can help you to feel <u>more involved</u> in society as a whole.

So you kick them in the shin and I'll steal the ball...

3) For <u>many</u> people, physical activity probably won't put a <u>roof over their heads</u>. But the <u>skills</u> you learn through exercise and sport can help you succeed at <u>work</u> as well as at the gym or on the playing field. Being <u>physically fit</u> can also help if your job involves <u>manual labour</u> or being <u>on your feet</u> all day.

Pumping iron with a grin on your face — serotonin' up...

These benefits are less obvious than those on the last page — especially the social health ones. But take your time and jot them down again and again until you've got them all stored in your head. Then try this Practice Question...

Q1   State **two** benefits of exercise to an individual's emotional health and well-being.   [2 marks]

Sedentary Lifestyle

Couch potatoes be warned — sitting still all day isn't good for you. In fact, a sedentary lifestyle can cause serious health issues. If you're sitting all day revising however, that's a different matter...

A *Sedentary Lifestyle* Includes *Little Physical Activity*

1) Lifestyle choices — like how you eat and drink, whether or not you smoke and how much sleep you get — will all have a knock-on effect on your fitness and your health.

2) If you have a sedentary lifestyle, it means you don't exercise enough:

> A SEDENTARY LIFESTYLE is one where there is irregular or no physical activity.

3) If you aren't active enough, you don't use up all the energy you get from food. Any excess energy is stored as fat, which increases your risk of becoming overweight or even obese (see below).

A *Sedentary Lifestyle* has *Many* Long-term Health Risks

A SEDENTARY LIFESTYLE CAN CAUSE:

- Lethargy (always feeling tired).
- Poor sleep.
- Emotional health problems like low confidence and self-esteem, poor body image and depression.
- Poor social health — it becomes hard to leave the home and socialise with others.
- Obesity (having a large amount of body fat).

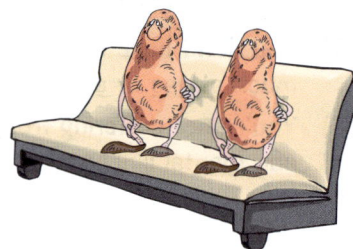

1) Obesity puts more strain on your cardiovascular system and decreases cardiovascular endurance.

2) Increased body fat can also lead to high cholesterol and fatty deposits in the arteries, making it harder for the heart to pump blood. This can lead to hypertension (high blood pressure) and the risk of strokes and coronary heart disease.

3) You are also more likely to develop type-2 diabetes if you are obese (see p54), and are more at risk of getting certain cancers.

4) Being overweight decreases flexibility, speed, power and agility, so affects your performance too.

> If you're inactive but skinny, you're still at risk of health problems.

You can use *BMI* to Determine if Someone is *Obese*

Your Body Mass Index (BMI) score is calculated using your height and weight:

Being UNDERWEIGHT means having a BMI of below 18.5.	Being a HEALTHY WEIGHT means having a BMI between 18.5 and 25.	Being OVERWEIGHT means having a BMI of 25 or over.	Being OBESE means having a BMI of 30 or over.

BMI doesn't take into account muscle mass or bone structure, so it can incorrectly classify healthy, muscular people as overweight or obese. See p61 for an example of some BMI data.

Sedentary? Not me — I get up and put the kettle on sometimes...

It is important to avoid a sedentary lifestyle by staying active. Make sure you learn all the definitions and health risks on this page, then hop to it and try this Exam Practice Question...

Q1 State **two** long-term health risks that are increased by a sedentary lifestyle.   [2 marks]

Diet and Nutrition

To stay healthy you need a balanced diet — this means getting the right amount of nutrients for your lifestyle.

You Should Eat a *Balanced Diet* to be *Healthy*

1) Eating a balanced diet is an important part of being healthy and helps you perform well in sport.

2) What makes up a balanced diet is slightly different for everyone, depending on how active you are.

> A balanced diet contains the best ratio of nutrients to match your lifestyle.

3) The 'best ratio' means the right amount of each nutrient in relation to the other nutrients. There isn't one type of 'superfood' that has everything your body needs — you need a mix of foods.

4) A balanced diet supports your lifestyle by providing the nutrients your body needs for energy, growth and hydration. It helps prevent health problems and injury, and to speed up recovery following exercise.

5) Your body needs large amounts of carbohydrates, fats and proteins. This pie chart shows the rough amounts of each that an average person should eat as part of a balanced diet:

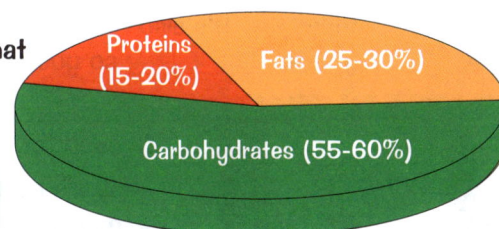

Proteins (15-20%)
Fats (25-30%)
Carbohydrates (55-60%)

CARBOHYDRATES

1) For most people, carbohydrates are the main source of energy for the body. Carbohydrates are vital for providing energy for your muscles during physical activity.

2) You can get simple ones like sugar, and complex ones, e.g. starch from pasta or rice.

Oh, I'm very complex y'know.

3) Whenever you eat carbohydrates, some will get used by the body straight away.

4) The rest gets stored in the liver and muscles, ready for when it's needed (or turned into fat).

PROTEINS

1) Proteins help the body grow and repair itself. They're vital for building and repairing muscles after exercise.

2) They're made from molecules called amino acids — your body can make new proteins from the amino acids in food.

3) Meat, fish, eggs and beans are all rich in protein.

FATS

1) Fats are made from molecules called fatty acids.

2) They provide more energy than carbohydrates for low-intensity exercise. They also help to keep the body warm and protect organs, which helps to prevent injury.

3) Some vitamins can only be absorbed by the body using fats.

4) Too many saturated fats can cause obesity.

Your *Energy Intake* and *Usage* Controls Your *Weight*

1) Energy from food is measured in calories (Kcal). On average, an adult male needs 2500 calories a day, and an adult female needs 2000 calories a day.

2) How much energy you need also depends on how much you use up through bodily processes (like breathing and digestion), daily activities and exercise. Age and height affect this too.

- If you take in more energy than you use, the spare energy is stored as fat, which causes you to gain weight.

- If you don't take in enough food to match the energy you need, your body makes up the difference by using up the energy stored in body fat and you lose weight.

- If you want to maintain a healthy weight, you need to make sure the energy you take in matches the energy you use up.

Energy In   Energy Out

A balanced diet — dead important for tight-rope walkers...

Make sure that you understand how carbohydrates, proteins and fats help you to do physical activity.

Q1   State **one** reason why carbohydrates are needed by the body.   [1 mark]

Diet and Nutrition

Good nutrition isn't just about eating the right amounts of carbohydrates, fats and proteins. Vitamins and minerals are important for maintaining body systems and general health, as is drinking plenty of water.

You need Small Amounts of Vitamins and Minerals

VITAMINS

1) Vitamins help your bones, teeth, skin and other tissues to grow. They're also needed for many of the body's chemical reactions, e.g. some are used in the processes that release energy from food.

2) Fat-soluble vitamins can be stored in the body. Here are a couple of examples:
   • Vitamin A — needed for your growth and vision.
   • Vitamin D — needed for strong bones so helps to prevent injury.

3) Water-soluble vitamins can't be stored, so you need to eat them regularly. For example:
   • Vitamin C — good for your skin and helps to hold your body tissues together. It's also really important for your immune system, so helps you to stay healthy so you can train and perform well.

Earl   Mini-earl

MINERALS

1) Needed for healthy bones and teeth, and to build other tissues.

2) Minerals help in various chemical reactions in the body:
   • Calcium — needed for strong bones and teeth, but also for muscle contraction.
   • Iron — used in making red blood cells, which carry oxygen round the body, e.g. to the muscles.

You also need fibre to keep your digestive system working properly — there's lots of fibre in fruit and vegetables.

Water is also Important for Good Health

WATER

1) Water is needed in loads of chemical reactions in the body. It's also used in sweat to help you cool down when your body temperature rises, e.g. through exercise. As well as sweating, you also lose water through your breath, urine and faeces.

2) If you don't drink enough to replace the water you've used or lost, you become dehydrated. This means your body doesn't have enough water to work well — it's not hydrated. This can cause:
   • Blood thickening — you guessed it, the blood gets thicker (more viscous). This makes it harder for the heart to pump the blood around — it has to work harder and beat faster. It also decreases the flow of oxygen to the muscles, so you can't perform as well in aerobic exercise, e.g. swimming.
   • Slower reactions and poor decision-making, as your brain needs water to function well. A boxer is less likely to be able to dodge an incoming punch.
   • An increase in body temperature, as without enough water the body can't sweat effectively. This can cause overheating and maybe even fainting through heat exhaustion.
   • Muscle fatigue and cramps, which could mean you have to stop doing an activity. Endurance athletes — like marathon runners — may not be able to finish their event.

3) Rehydration with water or sports drinks during and after physical activity helps avoid dehydration. This is important in endurance events and hot climates where you sweat more.

4) Sports drinks have sugar in them to replace the energy your muscles have used up. They also contain a bit of salt which helps the water rehydrate you quickly.

I won't include my joke about water — it just doesn't flow...

Make sure you understand why you need vitamins and minerals, the importance of water balance and the consequences of dehydration. Then time for a little Exam Practice Question? I think so...

Q1 Explain how dehydration could affect the performance of a sprinter.   [2 marks]

Somatotypes

Somatotype means the basic shape of your body. Your somatotype can affect your suitability for a particular sport. Learn the somatotypes and make sure you can identify which type suits what sport.

Somatotypes are *Body Types*

There are three basic somatotypes — ectomorph, mesomorph and endomorph.
Very few people are a perfect example of one of these body types — pretty much everyone is a mixture.
You can think of these basic somatotypes as extremes — at the corners of a triangular graph.

MESOMORPH — Muscular
ECTOMORPH — Thin
ENDOMORPH — Donald

Donald

② MESOMORPH
1) Wide shoulders and relatively narrow hips.
2) Muscular body.
3) Strong arms and thighs.
4) Not much body fat.

① ENDOMORPH
1) Wide hips but relatively narrow shoulders.
2) A lot of fat on the body, arms and legs.
3) Ankles and wrists are relatively thin.

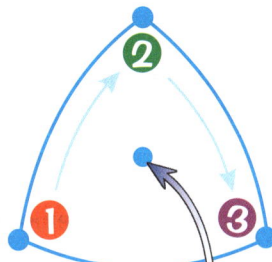

Mr Average would be in the middle of the graph.

③ ECTOMORPH
1) Narrow shoulders, hips and chest.
2) Not much muscle or fat.
3) Long, thin arms and legs.

Different Somatotypes suit *Different Sports*

Certain body types are better suited for certain sports — the right body type can give you an advantage.

Endomorphs are usually best at activities like wrestling and shot-put — where weight and a low centre of mass (see p22) can be an advantage.

E.g. in sumo wrestling, being heavy and having a low centre of mass makes it much harder for your opponent to throw you around the wrestling ring.

Ectomorphs suit activities like the high jump and long-distance running — where being light and having long legs is an advantage. They don't usually suit activities where strength is important.

E.g. high jumpers need to be light so they have less weight to lift over the bar. The taller the jumper, the shorter the distance they (and their centre of mass) have to travel to be able to get over the bar.

Mesomorphs are suited to most types of activity:
1) They're able to build up muscle relatively quickly and easily — which gives them an advantage in any activity where strength is important. E.g. sprinting, tennis, weightlifting...
2) Mesomorphs also have broad shoulders, which make it easier for them to be able to support weight using their upper body. This can be a huge advantage in activities like weightlifting and gymnastics.

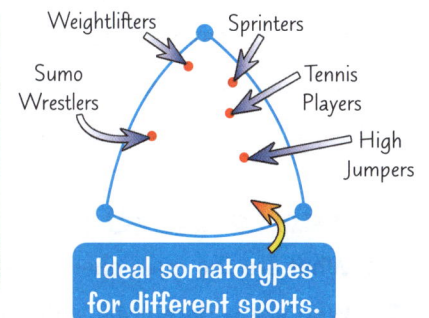

Weightlifters   Sprinters
Sumo Wrestlers   Tennis Players
                  High Jumpers

Ideal somatotypes for different sports.

What do you call a shape-shifting ghost? An ectomorph...

Remember — nearly everybody's a mixture of these basic body types. Learn the names well — it'd be a bad mistake to get the three somatotypes confused. Now, check you've got it with this Exam Practice Question...

Q1   State **one** example of a sport that an ectomorph is well suited to do. Justify your answer.   [2 marks]

Revision Questions for Section Six

That's it for Section Six. Give yourself a little time to digest all that information (ho ho ho), then fingers on buzzers for the Section Six revision questions...

- Try these questions and tick off each one when you get it right.
- When you've done all the questions for a topic and are completely happy with it, tick off the topic.
- The answers can all be found by looking back over pages 54 to 59.

Health, Fitness and Well-being (p54-55) ☑

1) Give two physical health benefits of physical activity.
2) How can exercise help you to avoid injury?
3) What effect does regular aerobic exercise have on blood pressure?
4) How can exercise make you feel good?
5) Give two social health benefits of sport.
6) Physical activity can increase your confidence. Is this a physical, emotional or social benefit?

Sedentary Lifestyle (p56) ☑

7) Define a 'sedentary lifestyle'. How is it connected to obesity?
8) What are two health risks associated with a sedentary lifestyle?
9) How might obesity affect performance in physical activity and sport?
10) Name the two factors that are needed to calculate Body Mass Index (BMI).
11) What weight classification is someone with a BMI score of 26? Why might this be misleading?

Diet and Nutrition (p57-58) ☐

12) What is a 'balanced diet'?
13) A balanced diet should contain what percentage of:
    a) carbohydrates?
    b) proteins?
    c) fats?
14) Name the nutrient that provides energy during high-intensity exercise.
15) How does protein help you to recover after exercise?
16) How many calories a day are required by: a) an average adult male, b) an average adult female?
17) What happens to your weight if you take in more energy than you use?
18) Give two reasons why the body needs vitamins.
19) Give one way that the body uses water.
20) Explain what happens to your blood when you become dehydrated.

Somatotypes (p59) ☑

21) What are the main characteristics of: a) an endomorph, b) a mesomorph, c) an ectomorph?
22) Why are endomorphs suited to wrestling and shot-put?
23) Why are ectomorphs suited to high jump and long-distance running?
24) Name a sport that mesomorphs are suited to and explain why.

Using Data

You've got to be comfortable with interpreting data displayed in graphs and tables. Luckily for you, these four pages will go through how you do it. And you thought you could get away from maths by taking PE...

There Are Two Different Types of Data

You can collect two different types of data — qualitative data and quantitative data:

The easiest way to remember the difference is 'quantitative' sounds like 'quantity' — which means 'number of'...

> Qualitative data describes something — it will be in words.

> Quantitative data measures something — it will be in numbers.

1) Qualitative data can be collected through observation — e.g. 'the team played well', 'the athlete is strong' or 'the weather was cold'.

2) Or you can interview people. E.g. asking an athlete how they're feeling before a race might give you answers like "confident" or "well-prepared".

3) It's less easy to analyse than data in numbers.

1) Quantitative data measures things — e.g. 'time taken to finish a race' or 'weight of an athlete'.

2) All the fitness tests (see pages 24-26) give quantitative data, as the results are numbers. You can also use surveys or questionnaires to collect quantitative data.

3) Quantitative data can be represented in tables and graphs, so it's easier to analyse.

You need to be able to Plot a Bar Chart from a Table

In the exam you might be asked to plot a bar chart using a table of data. You might know how to do this already, but it never hurts to go over it again. Below is a bar chart for the following data on BMI:

Number of students with each Body Mass Index (BMI) category

BMI category	Underweight	Healthy Weight	Overweight	Obese
No. of students	45	151	115	39

A scale for the values goes on the y-axis (up the side).

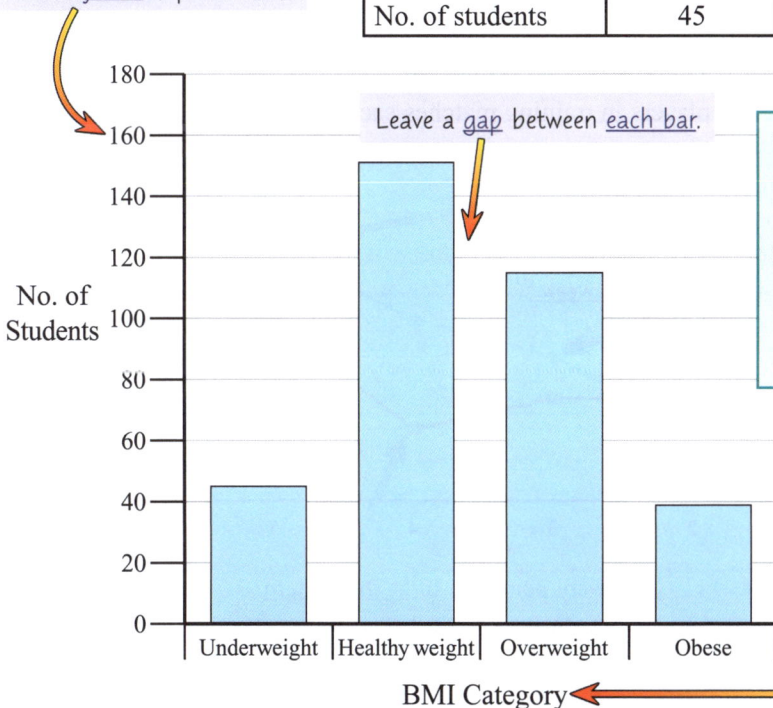

Leave a gap between each bar.

1) The height of each bar shows the data value for that category — the taller the bar, the bigger the value.

2) Plotting data as a bar chart makes it easy to compare categories. It's really easy to see the largest and smallest values.

The different categories go on the x-axis (along the bottom).

You get one mark just for labelling the axes — so don't forget...

Qualitatitative Qualatative Quiltative — Oh, I give up...

Just from my experiences writing this page, I can promise you that it's frustratingly easy to mix up the words qualitative and quantitative, so double-check you're using the right one. Exam Practice Question time...

Q1   State whether the data collected from the Illinois Agility Test is quantitative or qualitative data.   [1 mark]

Using Data

This page is all about line graphs — you need to know how to plot them and how to analyse them.

You can Plot a Line Graph from a Table

In the exam, you might be asked to plot a line graph from a table. You might know how to do this already, but it never hurts to go over it again... I seem to be having déjà vu.

Riyad's results for the stork stand test

Week	1	2	3	4	5	6
Time (secs)	12	13.5	13	15.5	18	21

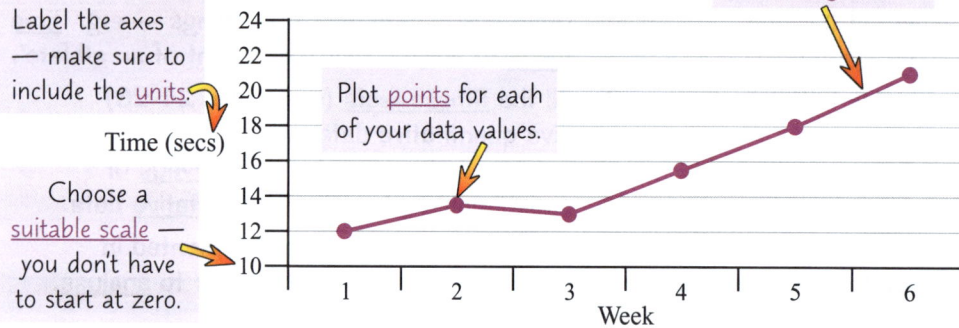

Join up the points with straight lines.

Label the axes — make sure to include the units.

Plot points for each of your data values.

Choose a suitable scale — you don't have to start at zero.

1) **Plotting** data as a **line graph** lets you see how things change over **time**.

2) Each **point** shows the value of the data at that time. You **join** the points up so you can easily see how the values are **changing**.

You can Analyse a Line Graph

To analyse a line graph you pick out certain bits of information and describe what's happening. You can:

- **Identify a specific point** — e.g. the **highest/lowest** value or the value at a **particular time**.
- **Compare data** — from **two sets of data** (e.g. 'males' and 'females') or **two times**.
- **Spot patterns** — whether the data is generally **increasing**, **decreasing** or staying the **same**.

Here's an example that shows how two sets of data (for two rugby players) can be analysed.

Number of tackles made by two rugby players in training matches each week

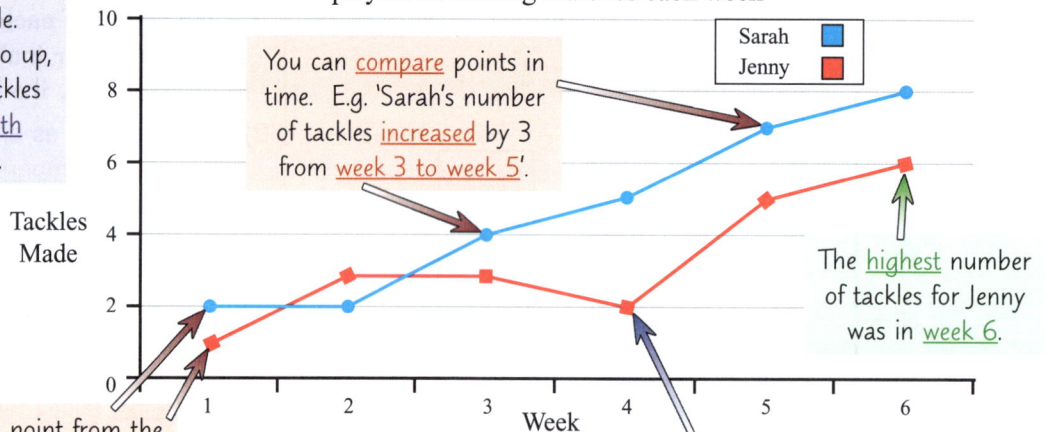

To spot patterns, look at the data as a whole. Both lines generally go up, so the number of tackles is increasing for both players over time.

You can compare points in time. E.g. 'Sarah's number of tackles increased by 3 from week 3 to week 5'.

The highest number of tackles for Jenny was in week 6.

You can compare a point from the two sets of data. E.g. 'Sarah made more tackles than Jenny in week 1'.

Not every point has to fit the pattern — sometimes you can get unusual results.

How do you analyse leopards? Spot patterns...

All these graphs... I'm starting to lose the plot (ho ho ho). If you can analyse graphs you'll breeze through any graph questions in the exam. Now, time to test those smarts with an Exam Practice Question...

Q1 Using the line graph about Sarah and Jenny above:
   a) Identify the week in which Jenny made two tackles. [1 mark]
   b) Identify which person had the bigger increase in tackles made from week 2 to week 6. [1 mark]

Using Data

You can analyse physical fitness by looking at data — on this page, you'll see how tables and bar charts can be used to analyse a person's fitness.

You can Analyse your Fitness over Time

1) You can measure components of fitness by doing regular fitness tests, and comparing the data you get over time.

2) You might have to describe what the data shows and say what this means about any training — i.e. if it's working or what changes are needed.

3) Here's an example of the kind of thing you might see in the exam:

Bryan is training to improve his cardiovascular endurance and his maximal strength.

Bryan

Bryan's Fitness Test Results

Fitness Test	Week					
	1	2	3	4	5	6
Multi-stage fitness test score (level)	7	7	8	9	9	10
Bench press one rep max (mass in kg)	65	66	65	66	64	65

The MSFT data shows that Bryan is gradually getting better at the test — he completes more levels over time. This suggests he's improving his cardiovascular endurance.

The one rep max data shows that the heaviest weight Bryan can bench press is staying about the same (approximately 65 kg). This suggests that his maximal strength is fairly constant.

For more on fitness testing see Section Three.

Another way to interpret your scores in fitness tests is to compare them to national averages or ratings tables for your age group or gender. For an example of this, see page 26.

Bar Charts can show Fitness Data

Remember that on a bar chart the heights of the bars show the data values. This means you can spot patterns by looking at how the heights of the bars change over time.

Week 1 has the tallest bar, so Bryan's resting heart rate was highest in week 1.

A bar chart showing Bryan's resting heart rate during each week of training

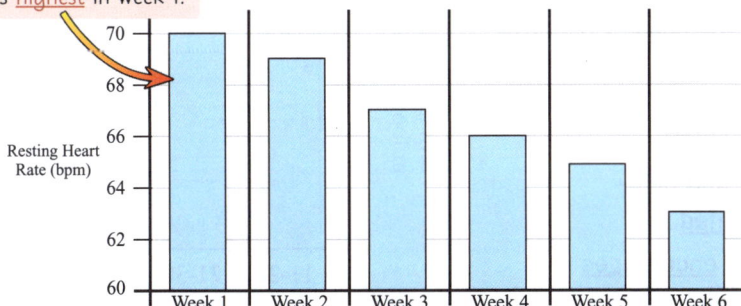

The pattern here is that Bryan's resting heart rate is decreasing each week. This suggests that his cardiovascular endurance must be improving, as his heart is pumping blood more efficiently.

Top of the charts again — give it up for the 'tallest bars'...

You can analyse data shown in tables and bar charts. To do this for fitness data, it might help to have another look over pages 24-25 to check you know all the fitness tests. Then try these Practice Questions...

Q1 Using the table above, identify the week in which Bryan got his lowest bench press one rep max. [1 mark]

Q2 Using the bar chart above, state what Bryan's resting heart rate was in week 4. [1 mark]

Using Data

More data? Well okay, go on then — I know how much you love it. This page is about delicious pie charts and other less delicious ways to interpret data. Needless to say, you have to learn it all, tasty or not so tasty.

Pie Charts *Show Proportions*

1) Pie charts are a good way to compare different categories — such as age groups or gender.

2) The amount of the whole chart a section takes up tells you the proportion in that category — the whole chart represents everybody.

3) It's important to remember that pie charts show proportions, not the actual number in each category.

The proportions are clearly shown on these pie charts — you can easily compare them to see that the netball club has the highest proportion of female members.

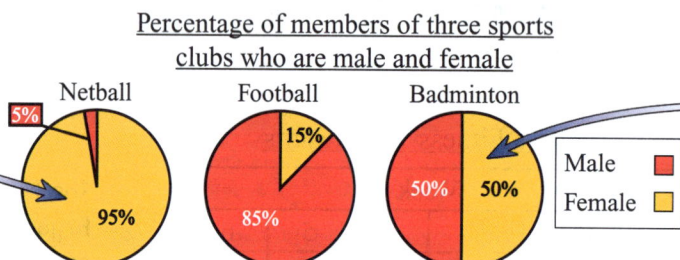

Percentage of members of three sports clubs who are male and female

Netball — 5%, 95%
Football — 15%, 85%
Badminton — 50%, 50%

Male ▮ (red)
Female ▮ (yellow)

You don't know the actual number of members. So you can't say things like 'the badminton club has more female members than the football club'.

4) You could be given one pie chart with lots of categories — e.g. a pie chart showing the proportion of money the government spends on different sports.

5) You don't need to be able to draw pie charts, just interpret them.

Interpret Data *in the Context of the Question*

To interpret data, you'll need to describe what it shows — you might also have to suggest possible reasons for the results using your PE knowledge.

EXAMPLE

The council of a large town carries out a survey to find out participation rates in football for different age groups. The bar chart below shows the results of the survey.

Interpret the bar chart and suggest one reason to explain the results.

E.g. The participation rate in football decreases as people get older.

There are lots of reasons that could explain the decrease in participation (see page 46), such as:

- The 11-20 category could be the highest because children might play football in PE at school.
- Older people may have other commitments — e.g. families, careers, etc.
- Football is a strenuous sport and older people could be physically limited.
- There might be a scheme that encourages younger people to play football.

Bar chart showing the participation rates in football at different ages in a town.

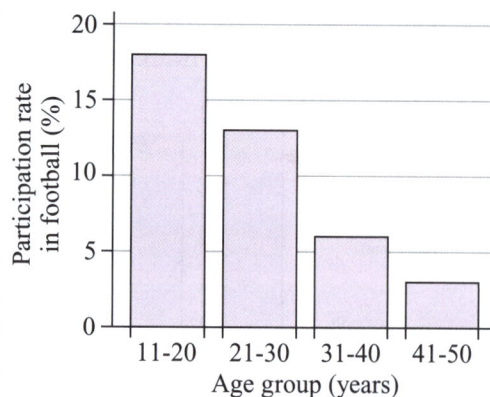

[Bar chart: Participation rate in football (%) on y-axis (0 to 20), Age group (years) on x-axis. 11-20: 18, 21-30: 13, 31-40: 6, 41-50: 3]

In the exam, any interpretation would get you the marks as long as it's suitable and you can justify it.

Mmmmmm — pie charts....

Remember, pie charts don't show actual numbers, only proportions. With that in mind, try this Practice Question...

Q1 Using the pie charts above, explain whether this statement is true, false or you can't tell:
'The netball club and the football club have the same number of members.' [2 marks]

Answering Exam Questions

Hurray — you made it to the end of the book. Now there's just the tiny matter (ahem) of the exams left to go. Here's what to expect in your exams and some exam tips to help you on your way to GCSE PE victory.

You'll Sit Two Exams for PE

Each paper will be worth 78 marks and will last 1 hour 15 minutes:

In total, your exams will make up 60% of your GCSE PE mark.

Paper 1

1) Paper 1 will test you on 'The human body and movement in physical activity and sport'.

2) It includes the topics:
   - Applied anatomy and physiology
   - Movement analysis
   - Physical training
   - Use of data

3) The first three topics are covered in sections 1-3 of this book (pages 1-36). 'Use of data' is in section 7 (pages 61-64).

Paper 2

1) Paper 2 will test you on 'Socio-cultural influences and well-being in physical activity and sport'.

2) It includes the topics:
   - Sports psychology
   - Socio-cultural influences
   - Health, fitness and well-being
   - Use of data

3) The first three topics are covered in sections 4-6 of this book (pages 37-60). 'Use of data' is in section 7 (pages 61-64).

There are Three Types of Question you could be asked

Multiple-Choice Questions — Shade the Right Oval

1) The multiple-choice questions give you a choice of four possible answers to the question. All you need to do is shade in the oval next to the correct answer. They're worth one mark each.

2) Make sure you only shade one oval — if you shade more than one you won't get the mark.

3) Don't worry if you make a mistake and want to change your answer. Just cross out the wrong answer, then shade in the oval next to your new answer.

There will be instructions on how to change your answer in the exam too.

4) If you don't know the answer to a question, guess. You don't lose marks for putting a wrong answer — if you guess, you've at least got a chance of getting it right.

Short-Answer Questions

1) Short-answer questions are usually worth between one and four marks.

2) Make sure you read the question carefully. For example, if you're asked for two influences, make sure you give two, otherwise you won't get all the marks.

3) To get the marks, you'll need to show your PE knowledge, apply it to a situation, or use it to analyse or evaluate something. In questions worth more marks, you might need to do a combination of these.

Extended Writing Questions

1) Extended writing questions are worth a whopping six or nine marks.

2) To answer these questions, as well as showing and applying your PE knowledge, you'll need to weigh up the advantages and disadvantages of something, or analyse how or why something happens.

3) At the end of your answer, you might need to write a conclusion where you make a judgement.

You will also be assessed on 'how well you write your answer', so make sure you do these things:

- Organise your answer — jot down what you want to cover in a quick plan before you start writing it. That way you can structure your answer well, and cover all the points you need to in a logical way.

- Answer the question being asked — stay focused on the topic you're asked about, and don't waffle about anything that's not relevant.

- Write in full sentences and use the correct spelling, grammar and punctuation.

- Use the correct PE vocabulary.

Answering Exam Questions

You get *Marks* for Meeting Different *Assessment Objectives*

1) Assessment objectives (AOs) are the things you need to do to get marks in the exams.

2) You'll be tested on three AOs:

> Assessment objective 1 (AO1) is all about demonstrating knowledge and understanding of a topic.
> 1) Questions that test AO1 usually ask you to state, define, describe, outline or identify something.
> 2) They could also get you to complete a table or draw / label a diagram or graph.

> Assessment objective 2 (AO2) is about applying knowledge and understanding of a topic to a context.
> 1) Questions that assess AO2 might ask you to explain why or how something happens.
> 2) You'll sometimes need to give examples or suggest reasons to back up your points.

> Assessment objective 3 (AO3) is about analysing and evaluating.
> 1) Questions that test AO3 often start with words like analyse, evaluate, discuss or justify.
> 2) Analysing just means breaking something down into parts or stages to explain it. This can include analysing data to explain what it shows.
> 3) To evaluate or discuss something, you will need to weigh up its advantages and disadvantages in the context given in the question.
> 4) Justifying something means giving reasons why it's sensible.

3) A lot of questions, especially extended writing questions, will test more than one assessment objective — for example, if a question tells you to evaluate something (AO3), you'll also need to demonstrate your knowledge of the topic (AO1) and apply it to the situation in the question (AO2).

In the Exams — *Read* the Questions and *Don't Panic*

1) Read every question carefully.

2) The number of marks each question is worth is shown next to it in brackets. This can be a good guide to the number of points you need to make and how long your answer should be.

> The number of answer lines given in a question can also be a good guide to how much to write.

3) Make sure your answers are clear and easy to read. If the examiner can't read your handwriting, they won't be able to give you any marks.

4) Don't panic — if you get stuck on a question, just move on to the next one. You can come back to it if you have time at the end.

Have a look at this Example *Question* and *Answer*

1) This example exam answer will show you how marks are awarded for the things you write:

15 **Figure 1** shows a performer taking part in archery.
Evaluate the importance of agility to the archer.

Figure 1

AO1 — *Agility is the ability to change body position or direction quickly and with control.*
AO2 — *Archers need to keep their body in a still, steady position so that they can aim accurately at the target.*
Therefore, agility is not an important component of fitness for an archer. ←AO3

[3 marks]

2) This answer gets one mark for each assessment objective it meets.

3) It meets AO1 by defining agility, AO2 by explaining what impact agility has on an archer, and AO3 by evaluating the importance of agility for the archer.

Answering Exam Questions

Answers

A note about answers and marks
The answers and mark schemes given here should be used mainly for guidance, as there may be many different correct answers to each question — don't panic if your answers are a bit different.

Section One — Anatomy and Physiology

Page 1 — The Skeletal System
Q1 E.g. Bones store minerals like calcium and phosphorus, which help maintain bone strength *[1 mark]*. Strong bones are essential for performance in physical activity and sport, as they reduce the chance of the bones becoming broken through the stress placed on them during exercise *[1 mark]*.

You could also say that these minerals also enable muscle contractions, which allow someone taking part in physical activity to perform the necessary sports movements.

Page 2 — The Skeletal System
Q1 **D** Tibia *[1 mark]*
Q2 **C** Talus *[1 mark]*

Page 3 — The Skeletal System
Q1 E.g. Rotation at the shoulder *[1 mark]* during a tennis serve *[1 mark]*.

Page 4 — The Skeletal System
Q1 E.g. During a netball pass, flexion at the elbow occurs in order to bring the ball backwards towards the player *[1 mark]*. Next, extension at the elbow occurs, straightening the arm and propelling the ball forward towards the target *[1 mark]*.

Q2 Cartilage covers the ends of bones that meet at joints *[1 mark]*, acting as a cushion between them *[1 mark]*. This allows a performer to use their joints for movement during sport without damage to the bones as they rub against each other *[1 mark]*.

Page 6 — The Muscular System
Q1 The hip flexors *[1 mark]*

When kicking a football, the hip flexors allow flexion at the hip so the entire leg swings forward.

Page 7 — The Cardiovascular System
Q1 E.g. The pulmonary artery carries deoxygenated blood *[1 mark]* to the lungs, where it becomes oxygenated *[1 mark]*. This is essential for physical activity and sport as this oxygenated blood can then be delivered to the muscles *[1 mark]* to provide the oxygen needed for exercise *[1 mark]*.

Page 8 — The Cardiovascular System
Q1 E.g. Capillaries have very thin walls *[1 mark]* which allow substances to pass through them easily *[1 mark]*. This means that oxygen can quickly be transferred from the capillaries to the muscles to release the energy needed for physical activity *[1 mark]*.

You could also say that the thin walls let carbon dioxide pass easily from the muscles back to the capillaries. Or you could have mentioned a different characteristic of capillaries, like their narrow diameters, and how this gives more time for oxygen and carbon dioxide to be exchanged with the muscles.

Page 9 — The Respiratory System
Q1 E.g. Deoxygenated blood becomes oxygenated through gas exchange between the capillaries containing the deoxygenated blood and the alveoli containing oxygen *[1 mark]*. Oxygen diffuses from an area of higher concentration (the alveoli) *[1 mark]* to an area of lower concentration (the deoxygenated blood) *[1 mark]*.

Page 10 — The Respiratory System
Q1 The lung volume shown at 'A' is tidal volume, which increases during exercise *[1 mark]*. This would be shown by larger 'peaks' on the spirometer trace *[1 mark]*.

Page 11 — Aerobic and Anaerobic Exercise
Q1 E.g. A 100 metre sprint would be an anaerobic exercise because it is a high intensity and short duration event *[1 mark]*. In the time taken to run 100 metres, the body systems would be unable to deliver oxygen quickly enough for the muscles to use aerobic respiration *[1 mark]*, so the muscles would release energy without oxygen *[1 mark]*.

Page 12 — Short-Term Effects of Exercise
Q1 E.g. A footballer experiencing muscle fatigue may be unable to sprint with the ball. This could make them less likely to score a goal *[1 mark]*.

Page 13 — Short-Term Effects of Exercise
Q1 Any two from: e.g. increased heart rate / increased stroke volume / increased cardiac output / increased blood pressure *[1 mark for each]*.

Q2 Vasodilation is the widening of blood vessels *[1 mark]*. This would occur in Katie's arms and legs when swimming to increase the amount of blood being delivered to them *[1 mark]*. The muscles would be supplied with sufficient oxygen to exercise aerobically *[1 mark]*.

Page 14 — Short-Term Effects of Exercise
Q1 a) 53 bpm *[1 mark]*
b) 167 bpm *[1 mark]*

Page 15 — Long-Term Effects of Exercise
Q1 E.g. Muscle hypertrophy means an increase in muscle thickness *[1 mark]*. This would benefit a performer participating in weightlifting because it would increase their strength *[1 mark]*, meaning they would be able to lift heavier weights *[1 mark]*.

Answers

Section Two — Movement Analysis

Page 17 — Lever Systems

Q1   E.g.

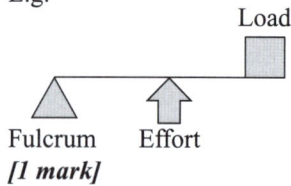

Load
Fulcrum   Effort
[1 mark]

When performing a squat, the knee is moving from flexion to extension, which uses a third class lever.

Page 18 — Planes and Axes of Movement

Q1   Frontal plane *[1 mark]* and sagittal axis *[1 mark]*

A star jump involves abduction and adduction of the arms and legs. These movements use the frontal plane and sagittal axis.

Section Three — Physical Training

Page 20 — Components of Fitness

Q1   E.g. An athlete might have a high level of fitness but train too much *[1 mark]*. This might cause them to get injured — reducing their health *[1 mark]*.

Page 21 — Components of Fitness

Q1   E.g. A rugby player uses power to kick the ball a long way *[1 mark]* and to tackle another player to the ground *[1 mark]*.

Remember that power is a combination of strength and speed. There are lots of other examples — e.g. jumping for the ball or sprinting for the try line.

Page 22 — Components of Fitness

Q1   E.g. Coordination is the ability to use two or more parts of the body together, efficiently and accurately *[1 mark]*. A boxer needs good hand-eye coordination to be able to throw a punch accurately *[1 mark]*.

Any example of using two or more body parts together in boxing is okay for the second mark.

Page 23 — Components of Fitness

Q1   E.g. Reaction time is the time taken to move in response to a stimulus *[1 mark]*.

E.g. Getting away quickly at the beginning of a sprint can mean the difference between winning and losing *[1 mark]*.

Page 25 — Fitness Testing

Q1   The handgrip dynamometer test is a test of (grip) strength *[1 mark]*. This is a suitable test for a rock climber *[1 mark]* as they need good strength to grip the holds on the wall *[1 mark]*.

Page 26 — Fitness Testing

Q1   **C** Average *[1 mark]*

Sarah's female and her time of 5.7 s falls between 5.60 s and 5.89 s — it's in the 'Average' column.

Page 27 — Principles of Training

Q1   E.g. A rower could train using a rowing machine *[1 mark]*, as this would work the same muscles as they use in their sport *[1 mark]*.

Page 28 — Principles of Training

Q1   E.g. You could get injured as the body hasn't had enough time to repair itself *[1 mark]*.

Page 29 — Training Target Zones

Q1 $220 - 35 = 185$ *[1 mark]*
185×0.8 *[1 mark]* $= 148$ bpm *[1 mark]*

The first mark is for finding the maximum heart rate (220 − age). The second mark is for using the right decimal for the threshold. And the last mark is for getting the maths right and getting the correct answer.

Page 30 — Training Methods

Q1   *This mark scheme gives examples of some points you might have made in your answer, and how many marks you'd get for making those points. You can still get full marks if you haven't written every individual point below, as long as the points you've made are detailed enough.*

You will get one mark for showing knowledge and understanding of continuous training, for example:

- Continuous training involves exercising at a steady, constant rate.
- It usually means exercising so that your heart rate is in your aerobic training zone.

You will get up to three marks if you also apply knowledge of continuous training to marathon runners and 100 m sprinters, for example:

- Continuous training improves aerobic fitness, which is important for aerobic activities like marathon running.
- It does not improve anaerobic fitness, so is not well suited to anaerobic activities like the 100 m sprint.

You will get up to six marks if you also evaluate how continuous training affects the performance of a marathon runner and a 100 m sprinter. You can include comparisons to other training methods. For example:

- Continuous training improves cardiovascular endurance — this helps marathon runners run the whole race at a steady, constant rate.
- It improves muscular endurance — leg muscles won't fatigue as quickly, so marathon runners can complete a race without stopping.
- Speed is more important than cardiovascular endurance for sprinters. Interval training — which involves maximum effort during the high-intensity bits — would be a more suitable training method for a 100 m sprinter. *[6 marks available in total]*

Page 31 — Training Methods

Q1   E.g. For strength training, an athlete needs to use a high weight (above 70% of their one rep max) *[1 mark]* and do a low number of reps (approximately three sets of 4-8 reps) *[1 mark]*.

Page 32 — Training Methods

Q1   E.g. Plyometric training increases power *[1 mark]*, which would help the basketball player to jump higher *[1 mark]*, increasing their ability to make interceptions *[1 mark]*.

One mark is for saying plyometric training improves power. One mark is for identifying an action that power helps with — e.g. jumping, sprinting, shooting. And one mark is for linking this to a specific basketball skill — e.g. lay-ups are easier when you can jump higher / sprinting faster allows you to get past opponents / a more powerful shot will help you to score three-point shots.

Answers

Page 33 — Training Methods

Q1 E.g. In pre-season training, performers need to improve the specific components of fitness they will need to compete *[1 mark]*. A high jumper could use plyometric training to improve their power, through exercises such as depth jumps *[1 mark]*. A high jumper needs power to achieve as much height on take-off as possible *[1 mark]*.

Page 34 — Preventing Injuries

Q1 E.g. The player should use taping/bracing to support joints *[1 mark]*. They should also complete an effective warm up before the match *[1 mark]*. During the match, the player should wear appropriate clothing/footwear *[1 mark]*.

Page 35 — Preventing Injuries

Q1 *This mark scheme gives examples of some points you might have made in your answer, and how many marks you'd get for making those points. You can still get full marks if you haven't written every individual point below, as long as the points you've made are detailed enough.*

You will get up to two marks for showing knowledge and understanding of a warm-up, for example:

- A warm-up includes light aerobic exercise to gradually increase your pulse rate.
- A warm-up includes stretching the muscles that will be used in the activity.
- A warm-up can include practice actions to prepare the muscles that will be used during the activity.

You will get up to four marks if you also apply knowledge of a warm-up to hockey, for example:

- Practising passing the ball in the warm-up helps prepare the shoulder and arm muscles for passing during the hockey match.
- Stretching the leg muscles in a warm-up is important as a hockey match involves a lot of jogging/running.

You will get up to nine marks if you also evaluate the importance of a warm-up in preventing injury in hockey. You can include comparisons with other methods of preventing injury in hockey. For example:

- Stretching of the leg muscles increases their flexibility which will help the player avoid injury when they lunge to reach the ball.
- Warm shoulder and arm muscles means there is less chance of injury with actions like passing or shooting.
- The light exercise eases the player's body into more intense exercise, which helps them avoid injury when they need to sprint to outrun other players during the hockey match.
- Protective equipment, such as gumshields and shin pads, is also necessary to prevent injuries. A warm up cannot protect you from being hit by a ball / hockey stick or from slipping over.
- In conclusion, a warm-up is absolutely vital before a hockey match to help prevent injury. However a warm-up alone is not sufficient to prevent all types of injury, so other measures must also be taken.

[9 marks available in total]

Section Four — Sport Psychology

Page 37 — Learning Skills

Q1 E.g. It could be classified as an open skill because you need to react to external factors, such as the position of the ball *[1 mark]*. It could be classified as a gross skill because you might have to run or dive to catch the ball, which uses powerful movements *[1 mark]*.

Page 38 — Goal Setting

Q1 E.g. This goal does not apply the 'measurable' principle *[1 mark]*. It is not measurable because it does not say how much faster the athlete would like to run *[1 mark]*.

You could also say that the goal doesn't apply the 'specific' principle for the same reason or the 'accepted' principle because the athlete's coach might not agree with her goal.

Page 39 — Guidance and Feedback

Q1 *This mark scheme gives examples of some points you might have made in your answer, and how many marks you'd get for making those points. You can still get full marks if you haven't written every individual point below, as long as the points you've made are detailed enough.*

You will get one mark for showing knowledge and understanding of the different types of guidance, for example:

- Verbal guidance includes instructions given in words.
- Verbal guidance involves a coach explaining how to perform a skill.
- Manual guidance involves a coach moving the performer's body through a technique.

You will get up to three marks if you also apply your knowledge of guidance to a beginner in golf, for example:

- Verbal guidance could include the coach telling the learner how to position their legs before swinging the club.
- Manual guidance could include the coach moving the learner's arms through a golf swing.
- Verbal and manual guidance could be used at the same time. For example, the coach could manually position the learner's hands on the club, while explaining how they should be positioned.

You will get up to six marks if you also evaluate which guidance type would be best for use with a beginner golfer, for example:

- Manual guidance can be useful for beginners as it gives them the feel of the correct technique. However, it can lead to the learner relying on it.
- Verbal guidance alone may be confusing for a beginner, as they may be unable to picture how a technique should feel due to their limited experience in golf.
- In conclusion, it would be best to combine verbal and manual guidance to improve a beginner's performance in golf. This would allow the learner to experience how golfing techniques feel while having them explained by the coach, to make sure they understand them.

[6 marks available in total]

Answers

Page 40 — Using Feedback

Q1 E.g. Praise is an example of positive feedback *[1 mark]*. This would teach the beginner that they should continue to use this stance on the snowboard *[1 mark]*, improving their future performance *[1 mark]*.

You could also say that this is extrinsic feedback, which is useful for beginners as they lack the knowledge needed to assess their own performance.

Page 41 — Mental Preparation

Q1 E.g. A football player may feel under a lot of pressure before taking a penalty, so could use mental rehearsal to help improve their confidence *[1 mark]*.

Page 42 — Emotion and Personality

Q1 **C** A medal *[1 mark]*

A medal is tangible because you can actually hold it and touch it. It's extrinsic because you'd get it from another person, not from yourself.

Section Five — Sport, Society and Culture

Page 44 — Influences on Participation

Q1 E.g. The attitudes your friends have about taking part in physical activity could influence your attitude *[1 mark]*. If they don't like sport, this could put pressure on you to also not take part in sport *[1 mark]*.

Page 45 — Influences on Participation

Q1 E.g. Local facilities might not provide many opportunities for disabled people to play sports, so you might be unable to participate *[1 mark]*.

Page 46 — Influences on Participation

Q1 Any two from: e.g. Students could be allowed to choose from a range of activities / the school could invest in new facilities, equipment or changing rooms / the school could offer non-competitive options in PE / the school could bring in outside agencies to help with coaching and development *[1 mark for each]*.

Page 47 — Commercialisation of Sport

Q1 E.g. Media coverage of sports creates role models *[1 mark]*. This can inspire people watching the sport to participate *[1 mark]*. Media coverage of a sport allows it to reach a much larger audience *[1 mark]*. This means that more people will become aware of the sport and learn about it, which may encourage them to take it up *[1 mark]*.

With each point, make sure you say enough to get two marks by saying how the media's coverage of sport encourages people to take part.

Page 48 — Commercialisation of Sport

Q1 E.g. Sponsorship by a fast-food company would have a positive impact because it would give the team more money *[1 mark]*. This would allow them to buy more equipment or improve facilities *[1 mark]*. However, as it is an under-12's team, the young players and supporters may be influenced to eat more fast food *[1 mark]*, which could lead to an increased risk of obesity *[1 mark]*.

Page 49 — Technology in Sport

Q1 *This mark scheme gives examples of some points you might have made in your answer, and how many marks you'd get for making those points. You can still get full marks if you haven't written every individual point below, as long as the points you've made are detailed enough.*

You will get up to two marks for showing knowledge and understanding of technology in sport, for example:

- New materials can be used to make sportspeople's equipment and clothing more effective.
- Video recordings and training software can help coaches analyse performers' movement.
- Technology has been introduced to help referees and umpires.

You will get up to four marks if you also give examples of technology being used in sporting activities, for example:

- Using new materials to make swimming costumes has improved the performances of swimmers.
- Using software to analyse an athlete's movement in the 100 m sprint allows the athlete and their coach to fine-tune their technique.
- The use of Hawk-Eye / the Decision Review System in cricket means players can challenge an umpire's call.

You will get up to nine marks if you also justify the impact of technology on sport, for example:

- Use of analysis technology in training can lead to new levels of achievement in sport. However, this technology is expensive, so people who can't afford it might not be able to fairly compete with those with more money.
- Sponsors could use the breaks in play caused by the use of technology to play adverts. More sponsorship means more money for sport which can be used to improve facilities and participation.
- Using technology to support officials makes sport fairer as it helps ensure correct decisions are made and improves the sport for spectators and players.
- Some umpires in cricket are concerned that by using technology to support their decisions, this undermines their authority on the pitch, which could lead to players not respecting their decisions.
- Better swimming costumes have helped swimmers set new world records, which has made the sport very exciting. However, it does run the risk of making swimming more about the technology involved in the costume, and less about the ability of the swimmers themselves.
[9 marks available in total]

71

Answers

Page 50 — Sporting Behaviour

Q1 E.g. Sportsmanship means being honest, sticking to the rules and treating your opponents with respect *[1 mark]*, whereas gamesmanship involves bending the rules, without actually breaking them *[1 mark]*.

Page 51 — Performance-Enhancing Drugs

Q1 E.g. Beta blockers might be used by an archer because they have a calming effect and steady shaking hands *[1 mark]*, which will help the archer keep steady as they take aim and shoot *[1 mark]*.

There are a few different performance-enhancing drugs that might improve an archer's performance. The first mark comes from explaining what the drug does. And the second mark comes from applying that effect to archery.

Page 52 — Spectator Behaviour

Q1 Any two from: e.g. Rivalries between fans / media hyping up the game so people take it too seriously / drinking or drug taking amongst fans / frustration with the way the game is going or decisions made by officials / a gang culture meaning fans feel less responsible for their actions / peer pressure from other supporters to join in rowdy and violent behaviour *[1 mark for each]*.

Section Six — Health, Fitness and Well-being

Page 54 — Health, Fitness and Well-being

Q1 Any two from: e.g. Improves cardiovascular endurance so you can exercise more intensely and for longer / muscles and bones get stronger, reducing the chance of injury / everyday tasks are easier and you're less likely to become fatigued / reduces the risk of illnesses, such as diabetes, so you can continue to exercise *[1 mark for each]*.

Page 55 — Health, Fitness and Well-being

Q1 Any two from: e.g. Exercise relieves stress/tension / it can help you learn to cope with pressure/manage emotions / it can increase self-esteem and confidence / it can increase your levels of serotonin, which makes you feel good / gains in physical health can help to improve your body-image *[1 mark for each]*.

You need to give two benefits for two marks — so you don't need to go into any depth.

Page 56 — Sedentary Lifestyle

Q1 Any two from: e.g. Obesity / depression / high blood pressure (hypertension) / coronary heart disease / diabetes *[1 mark for each]*.

Page 57 — Diet and Nutrition

Q1 Any one from: e.g. Carbohydrates provide energy for your muscles during physical activity / the body can use carbohydrates for energy straight away / carbohydrates can be stored in the body until they are needed *[1 mark]*.

Page 58 — Diet and Nutrition

Q1 Any two from: e.g. Dehydration can cause slower reactions, so a sprinter might not leave the starting block straight away / muscle fatigue and cramps could mean the sprinter has to stop the race / increased body temperature could cause the sprinter to faint *[1 mark for each]*.

Page 59 — Somatotypes

Q1 E.g. Ectomorphs are well suited to being long-distance runners *[1 mark]*, because being light and having long legs means they can run very efficiently *[1 mark]*.

Section Seven — Using Data

Page 61 — Using Data

Q1 Quantitative data *[1 mark]*

The test measures time (in seconds), which is a number.

Page 62 — Using Data

Q1 a) Week 4 *[1 mark]*
b) Sarah *[1 mark]*

Sarah had an increase of 6, from 2 tackles to 8. Jenny only increased by 3, from 3 tackles to 6.

Page 63 — Using Data

Q1 Week 5 *[1 mark]*
Q2 66 bpm *[1 mark]*

Page 64 — Using Data

Q1 You can't tell whether the statement is true or false *[1 mark]*, because the pie charts don't give the total number of members in each club *[1 mark]*.

This can be confusing because the pie charts are the same size.

Answers

72

Glossary

abduction	Movement <u>away</u> from an imaginary <u>centre line</u> through the body.
ability	A person's set of <u>traits</u> that control their <u>potential</u> to <u>learn a skill</u>.
adduction	Movement <u>towards</u> an imaginary <u>centre line</u> through the body.
aerobic exercise	'With oxygen'. When exercise is <u>not too fast</u> and is <u>steady</u>, the heart can supply all the oxygen that the working muscles need.
agility	The <u>ability</u> to change <u>body position</u> or <u>direction</u> quickly and with control.
alveoli	Small <u>air bags</u> in the <u>lungs</u> where gases are exchanged.
anaerobic exercise	'Without oxygen'. When exercise duration is <u>short</u> and at <u>high intensity</u>, the heart and lungs can't supply blood and oxygen to muscles as fast as the cells need them.
antagonistic muscle pair	A pair of muscles that work <u>together</u> to bring about movement. As one muscle <u>contracts</u> (the <u>agonist</u> or <u>prime mover</u>) the other <u>relaxes</u> (the <u>antagonist</u>).
arousal	A person's level of mental and physical <u>alertness</u>.
axis of movement	An <u>imaginary line</u> that the body or a body part can <u>move around</u>.
balance	The ability to keep the body's <u>centre of mass</u> over a <u>base of support</u>.
balanced diet	A diet that contains the best <u>ratio</u> of <u>nutrients</u> to match your <u>lifestyle</u>.
basic skill	A <u>simple</u> skill which <u>doesn't</u> need much <u>thought</u> or <u>decision-making</u> to do, e.g. running.
blood cell	Component of <u>blood</u>. There are <u>red blood cells</u> (which carry oxygen and carbon dioxide) and <u>white blood cells</u> (which fight disease).
blood pressure	How <u>strongly</u> the blood presses against the walls of <u>blood vessels</u>.
blood vessel	Part of the cardiovascular system that <u>transports blood</u> around the body. The three main types are <u>arteries</u>, <u>veins</u> and <u>capillaries</u>.
Body Mass Index (BMI)	A <u>score</u> used to determine whether a person is <u>underweight</u>, a <u>healthy weight</u>, <u>overweight</u> or <u>obese</u>.
calorie	A <u>unit</u> used to measure the amount of <u>energy in food</u>. It's often shortened to <u>Kcal</u>.
cardiac output	The <u>volume of blood</u> pumped by each ventricle in the heart per minute.
cardio-respiratory system	The combination of the <u>cardiovascular</u> and <u>respiratory</u> systems working together to get <u>oxygen</u> into the body tissues and <u>carbon dioxide</u> out of them.
cardiovascular endurance	The ability of the <u>heart</u> and <u>lungs</u> to <u>supply oxygen</u> to the working muscles.
cardiovascular system	The <u>organs</u> responsible for <u>circulating blood</u> around the body.
closed skill	A skill performed in a <u>predictable environment</u> — it's not affected by external factors.
commercialisation	<u>Managing sport</u> in a way designed to make <u>profit</u>, e.g. through <u>sponsorship</u> and the <u>media</u>.
complex skill	A skill which needs <u>lots of thought</u> or <u>decision-making</u> to do, e.g. a volley in football.
concentric contraction	A type of isotonic muscle contraction where a muscle contracts and <u>shortens</u>.
connective tissue	Body tissue that <u>holds</u> other body tissues (e.g. muscles and bones) <u>together</u>.
contract to compete	An <u>unwritten agreement</u> between competitors to <u>comply</u> with all the rules.
cool-down	<u>Light exercise</u> and <u>stretching</u> done <u>after exercise</u> to return your body to resting levels.

Glossary

Glossary

coordination	The ability to use <u>two or more</u> parts of the body <u>together</u>, efficiently and accurately.
data	<u>Information</u> — in <u>words</u> or <u>numbers</u> that can be shown in <u>graphs</u> and <u>tables</u>. Data can be <u>quantitative</u> (numbers) or <u>qualitative</u> (words).
delayed onset of muscle soreness (DOMS)	<u>Soreness</u> in the muscles in the <u>days after exercise</u>.
diffusion	The process of <u>substances</u> (e.g. oxygen) <u>moving</u> from a place where there is a <u>higher concentration</u> to a place where there is a <u>lower concentration</u>.
dorsiflexion	<u>Flexion</u> at the <u>ankle</u> by lifting the toes.
eccentric contraction	A type of isotonic muscle contraction where a muscle contracts and <u>lengthens</u>.
expiratory reserve volume (ERV)	The amount of <u>extra air</u> that can be <u>breathed out</u> after breathing out normally.
extension	<u>Opening a joint</u>, e.g. straightening the leg at the knee.
externally-paced skill	A skill that starts because of <u>external factors</u> which also <u>control the pace</u> of the skill.
feedback	Information about <u>how you did</u> — can be <u>intrinsic</u> (from yourself) or <u>extrinsic</u> (from other sources).
fine skill	A skill using <u>small muscle groups</u> for <u>precise</u> movements requiring <u>accuracy</u> and <u>coordination</u>.
fitness	The ability to meet/cope with the <u>demands</u> of the <u>environment</u>.
flexibility	The amount of <u>movement</u> possible at a <u>joint</u>.
flexion	<u>Closing a joint</u>, e.g. bending the arm at the elbow.
gamesmanship	Gaining an <u>advantage</u> by using tactics that <u>seem unfair</u>, but aren't against the rules.
gross skill	A skill involving <u>powerful movements</u> performed by <u>large muscle groups</u>.
guidance	<u>Information</u> or <u>help</u> in learning a skill. Guidance can be visual, verbal, manual or mechanical.
health	A state of complete <u>physical</u>, <u>mental</u> and <u>social well-being</u> and not merely the absence of disease or infirmity.
heart rate	The number of times your <u>heart beats</u> in one minute. It is measured in <u>beats per minute</u> (bpm).
hooliganism	<u>Rowdy</u>, <u>aggressive</u> and <u>sometimes violent</u> behaviour of fans and spectators of sport.
hydration	Having the <u>right</u> amount of <u>water</u> for the body to function properly. If you have <u>too little</u> water, you're <u>dehydrated</u>.
inspiratory reserve volume (IRV)	The amount of <u>extra air</u> that can still be <u>breathed in</u> after breathing in normally.
isometric contraction	When a muscle stays the <u>same length</u> as it contracts.
isotonic contraction	When a muscle <u>changes length</u> as it contracts.
joint type	<u>Ball and socket</u> and <u>hinge</u> joints both allow a different <u>range of movement</u>.
lactic acid	A <u>waste product</u> produced during <u>anaerobic respiration</u>, making the muscles feel tired (fatigued).
lever system	A system that allows the body's muscles to move the bones in the skeleton. A lever system can be <u>first</u>, <u>second</u> or <u>third class</u>, and is made up of a lever arm, effort, fulcrum and load.
mechanical advantage	A measure of how <u>efficient</u> a lever is at moving <u>heavy loads</u>.

Glossary

the media	Organisations involved in <u>mass communication</u> — e.g. through television, radio, newspapers and the Internet.
muscular endurance	The ability to <u>repeatedly</u> use the <u>muscles</u> over a long time, without getting <u>tired</u>.
musculo-skeletal system	The combination of the <u>muscular</u> and <u>skeletal systems</u> working together to allow movement.
obesity	Being <u>obese</u> means having a <u>BMI</u> score of <u>30 or over</u>.
open skill	A skill performed in a <u>changing environment</u>, where a performer has to <u>react</u> and adapt to <u>external factors</u>.
plane of movement	Imaginary <u>surface</u> used to describe the <u>direction</u> of movement. E.g. sagittal, transverse and frontal.
plantar flexion	<u>Extension</u> at the <u>ankle</u> by pointing the toes.
power	A combination of <u>speed</u> and <u>strength</u>.
reaction time	The time taken to <u>move</u> in <u>response</u> to a stimulus.
residual volume	The amount of <u>air left</u> in the lungs after the <u>most possible</u> air has been <u>breathed out</u>.
respiratory system	The <u>organs</u> in the body used for <u>breathing</u>.
rotation	Movement of the body or a body part in a <u>clockwise</u> or <u>anticlockwise</u> motion.
sedentary lifestyle	A lifestyle with <u>irregular</u> or <u>no physical activity</u>.
self-paced skill	A skill <u>controlled</u> by the <u>performer</u> — they decide when and how quickly it's done.
SMART	The <u>five principles of goal setting</u> — <u>specific</u>, <u>measurable</u>, <u>accepted</u>, <u>realistic</u> and <u>time-bound</u>.
socio-economic group	A way of grouping people based on their <u>job</u>, how much <u>money</u> they have and <u>where they live</u>, e.g. 'working class is' a socio-economic group.
somatotype	A person's <u>body type</u> based on their <u>body shape</u> and the amount of <u>muscle</u> and <u>fat</u> they have.
speed	The <u>rate</u> at which someone is able to <u>move</u>, or to <u>cover</u> a <u>distance</u> in a given amount of <u>time</u>.
spirometer trace	A <u>graph</u> produced by a spirometer machine which can be used to measure <u>lung volumes</u>.
sponsorship	The provision of <u>money</u>, <u>equipment</u>, <u>clothing/footwear</u>, or <u>facilities</u> to an individual, team or event in return for some <u>financial gain</u>.
SPORT	The <u>four principles of training</u> — <u>specificity</u>, <u>progressive overload</u>, <u>reversibility</u> and <u>tedium</u>.
sportsmanship	Playing <u>within the rules</u>, upholding the <u>spirit of the game</u> and using <u>sports etiquette</u>.
strength	The amount of <u>force</u> that a <u>muscle</u> or <u>muscle group</u> can apply against a <u>resistance</u>.
stroke volume	The <u>volume of blood</u> pumped with each <u>heartbeat</u> by each ventricle in the heart.
synovial joint	Where two or more <u>bones</u> are <u>joined together</u> in a joint capsule containing synovial fluid.
tidal volume	The <u>amount of air</u> that is breathed in or out in <u>one breath</u>.
training season	Training programmes with different aims depending on whether it's <u>before</u>, <u>during</u> or <u>after</u> the period when sport competition takes place.
training target zone	The range where <u>training</u> is at the right <u>intensity</u> — can be either <u>aerobic</u> (60-80% of maximum heart rate) or <u>anaerobic</u> (80-90% of maximum heart rate).
warm-up	<u>Preparing</u> your body for <u>exercise</u> with pulse-raising activity, stretching and practice actions.

Index

Index